# *Tomorrow the Pacific*

## H. Edward English

*Observation 34*
*C.D. Howe Institute*

C.D. Howe Institute publications are available from:

Renouf Publishing Company Limited, 1294 Algoma Road, Ottawa, Ontario K1B 3W8; telephone: (613) 741-4333; fax (613) 741-5439; and from Renouf's stores at: 61 Sparks Street, Ottawa (613) 238-8985; and 211 Yonge Street, Toronto (416) 363-3171

Institute publications are also available in microform from:

Micromedia Limited, 158 Pearl Street, Toronto, Ontario M5H 1L3

For trade book orders, please contact:

McGraw-Hill Ryerson Limited, 330 Progress Avenue, Scarborough, Ontario M1P 2Z5; telephone (416) 293-1911

**Canadian Cataloguing in Publication Data**

English, H. Edward (Harry Edward), 1924–
    Tomorrow the Pacific

(Observation, ISSN 0826-9947 ; 34)
Includes bibliographical references.
ISBN 0-88806-257-5

1. Pacific Area - Economic conditions.  2. Pacific
Area - Commerce.  3. Canada - Foreign economic
relations - Pacific Area.  4. Pacific Area - Foreign
economic relations - Canada. I. C.D. Howe
Institute.  II. Title.  III. Series: Observation
(C.D. Howe Institute. English).

HC681.E63 1991      338.9'009182'3      C91-093576-9

# Contents

# Foreword

One of the most striking developments in the years since the end of World War II has been the shift in the world's economic axis that has resulted in the increasing dominance of the countries on the Pacific Rim. At more than US$9 *trillion*, the combined gross national product of these countries is nearly double that of Europe, and their economies are growing at a faster rate than those of Europe.

The vast and diverse Pacific region is dominated by two economic superpowers, the United States and Japan. There is concern, therefore, that rival blocs will coalesce around these two countries, and that the Pacific will become a region of economic conflict, rather than of cooperation. Attention thus needs to focus on the development of institutions, such as the Pacific Economic Cooperation Conference (PECC), whose purpose is to foster cooperation among the region's economic players, large and small, developed and developing countries alike. It is clearly in Canada's interest to promote this option.

Few people are better able to examine these issues than the study's author, H. Edward English, Professor of Economics at Carleton University and the Canadian member of the International Steering Committee of the Pacific Trade and Development Conference, whose members helped to establish PECC in 1980. The book was edited and prepared for publication by Barry A. Norris with the assistance of Brenda Palmer. As with all Institute publications, the conclusions presented here are those of the author and do not necessarily reflect the views of the Institute's members or Board of Directors.

Thomas E. Kierans
President and
Chief Executive Officer

# Preface

This book's title, some would say, should include a question mark. This view is based on Canadians' obvious preoccupation with continental affairs — recently extended to the consequences of closer economic relations between Mexico and the United States and their implications for Canada — and with the more traditional European arena. Since late 1989, the dramatic events in Eastern Europe and, more recently, in the Persian Gulf have drawn Canadian policymakers, and those responsible for Canada's foreign relations, once more into other concerns and challenges.

But what of the Pacific? The president of Mexico has enroled his children in a Japanese immersion program. President Gorbachev's planned trip to Japan in 1991 may very well be accompanied by an announcement that the Soviet Union intends to return to Japan four islands it has occupied since the end of World War II, an act which would remove a significant obstacle to the expansion of economic and other relations between the two countries.

Canada's "trade development strategy" continues, in principle, to give equal priority to Asia-Pacific relations. Ottawa remains firmly committed to the preservation and strengthening of multilateral institutions, especially the General Agreement on Tariffs and Trade (GATT). This position is now complemented by a three-track, or three-pillar, strategy that gives equal attention to North America, Europe, and the Pacific.

In North America, the main objective is to ensure the success of the bilateral free trade agreement and to identify an appropriate Canadian role in free trade talks between the United States and Mexico. In Europe, apart from the Uruguay Round of the GATT, Canada's initiatives will be purely bilateral.

The Pacific offers more scope for both bilateral and regional initiatives. It is the region of the most rapid economic growth, and it is the one that is most representative of the interests of countries at all stages of development. Furthermore, the development of these countries has been based on a firm commitment to outward-oriented trade and investment strategies. Cooperation among these countries is already preserving the multilateral trading system and the flow of long-term investment funds and technology.

It is no longer news that more trade crosses the Pacific than the Atlantic. It is estimated that the value of that trade may well increase during the 1990s from the current $300 billion to more than $500 billion. By the end of the decade, Pacific Asia alone is likely to account for 60 percent of the world's population, 50 percent of global production, and 40 percent of global consumption. With the expansion of regional consensus-forming institutions to include Latin American countries, and the Soviet Union's interest in participating in these same institutions, the region's weight in world economic affairs should be further enhanced.

The preparation of this monograph owes much to all those who have participated in the work of the Pacific Trade and Development Conferences over the past 20 years, and to those from business and government with whom I have been associated during the evolution of the Pacific Economic Cooperation Conferences over the past ten years.

I would also like to express my appreciation to referees who commented most constructively on an earlier draft. Finally, special thanks must go to Lorne T. Woods, a Canadian doctoral graduate from Australian National University, for his definitive work on the evolution of Pacific institutions. The Bibliography to be found at the end of this study is mostly taken from a larger survey of the literature included in his doctoral dissertation.

H. Edward English

# 1

## The Pacific:
## Economic Colossus?

*Both coasts of the Pacific Ocean will soon be as populated,
as open to commerce and as industrialized as the coast from
Boston to New Orleans is now. Then the Pacific Ocean will
play the same role as the Atlantic Ocean does now and as
the Mediterranean did in antiquity and in the Middle Ages
— the role of a great water highway of world commerce —
and the Atlantic Ocean will decline to the level of an inland
sea, as the Mediterranean is now.*

Karl Marx and Friedrich Engels, 1850 [1]

This startling forecast was more accurate than some of the
more famous projections on the evolution of human society by
these two founders of communism. They were commenting on
the probable consequences of the California gold rush; like
many modern futurists, they argued a good case on rather
simplistic grounds. Most people today would stress the human
resources, skills, and technology of the Pacific as the keys to
its burgeoning economic prosperity and the dynamism of its

---

[1] Karl Marx and Friedrich Engels, "The Global Consequences of the Discovery
of Gold in California," *Neue Reinische Zeitung, Politisch-Okonomische Revue,*
January-February 1850.

trade and investment links, Japan is the symbol of the primacy of the human factor. But other Pacific countries' natural resources, more useful than gold, have created the ingredients of Japan's industrial success and the markets for its products. Technology has also contributed the jet aircraft, containerized and specialized ships, and the satellites and other telecommunications marvels that lubricate the Pacific boom.

Variety is the spice of the Pacific. An introduction to Pacific economies and societies illustrates the great variety of the region (see Table 1). The economic characteristics of the region can be summarized as follows:

- the great variety in the size of its economies — ranging from the world's two largest (the United States and Japan) to the tiny island states of the Pacific Ocean; note that Canada has a higher gross domestic product (GDP) than China;
- the great differences in per capita income, even among the larger countries of the region (compare China and the United States) and between neighboring states (see China and Hong Kong, or Indonesia and Singapore);
- the substantial differences in growth records, both among countries and over time; it should be noted. however, that the average rates in the region exceed those sustained in most other parts of the world — for example, between 1984 and 1988, none of the four largest members of the European Community exceeded 3.3 percent in average annual growth;
- the impressive growth of trade flows for most countries of the region, which is a primary reason for the variations in GDP performances — generally, the newly industrialized economies (NIEs) have had superior rates of growth in the past two decades, although in 1989 the resource-rich Southeast Asian countries experienced higher growth rates as a result of the recovery of markets for primary products.

**Table 1**

*Economic Indicators of the Variety of the Pacific Region*

| | GDP in 1987 (US$ billions) | GDP per capita 1987 | GDP growth 1986–87 | Real GDP growth, 1989 | Real export growth, 1989 | Real import growth 1989 |
|---|---|---|---|---|---|---|
| *Developed countries* | | | | | | |
| United States | $4,488.6 | $18,413 | 2.9% | 3.0% | 11.1% | 6.1% |
| Japan | 2,384.5 | 19,530 | 3.4 | 5.1 | 12.2 | 11.6 |
| Canada | 405.1 | 15,794 | 3.0 | 2.9 | -0.9 | 7.2 |
| Australia | 193.8 | 11,925 | 3.1 | 4.9 | 3.7 | 20.6 |
| New Zealand | 27.7 | 8,524 | n.a | 1.4 | 0.3 | 17.4 |
| *East Asia* | | | | | | |
| China | 245.9 | 230 | 5.8 | 3.9 | 5.1 | 5.6 |
| South Korea | 121.3 | 2,883 | 11.4 | 6.7 | -5.2 | 14.2 |
| Taiwan | 94.6 | 4,844 | 10.8 | 7.2 | 4.9 | 9.1 |
| Hong Kong | 46.5 | 8,297 | 12.6 | 2.5 | 10.2 | 8.9 |
| *Southeast Asia* | | | | | | |
| Indonesia | 75.2 | 451 | 3.2 | 5.9 | 15.0 | 11.6 |
| Thailand | 47.1 | 879 | 4.9 | 11.0 | 28.7 | 29.0 |
| Philippines | 34.3 | 599 | 3.8 | 5.5 | 11.7 | 22.5 |
| Malaysia | 32.0 | 1,935 | 3.2 | 8.5 | 18.0 | 13.1 |
| Singapore | 19.9 | 7,623 | 5.3 | 9.2 | 11.2 | 11.5 |

Note: GDP data have been converted into U.S. dollars on an exchange-rate basis. If purchasing power parity adjustments are made, the United States would register a higher per capita real income relative to Japan, at least up to 1988.

Sources: *Asia-Pacific Report 1989* (Honolulu: East-West Centre, 1989); Pacific Economic Cooperation Conference, *Pacific Economic Outlook, 1990–1991* (Washington, D.C., 1990).

In general, the variety of the Pacific can be further characterized by observing that the region includes two economies with a highly diversified economic base (the United States and China), three with an economic base founded primarily on manufacturing activity (Japan, South Korea, and Taiwan), two that are heavily oriented toward service sectors (Hong Kong and Singapore), and seven that are very dependent on the production and trade of resources (Australia, Canada, and New Zealand among the developed countries, and Indonesia, Malaysia, the Philippines, and Thailand among the developing countries and NIEs. With regard to Pacific relations, variety of this kind becomes a foundation for complementarity and trade.

Social and political dimensions give additional flavor to the Pacific mix. Three countries — Japan, South Korea,,and Thailand — have languages that are almost unique. In four others, English is the dominant language. Four use Chinese or a Chinese-English mix, and the Malay language family is predominant in three. Religious affiliations are equally diverse, with five countries that are predominantly Christian, five that are Buddhist or that practice a combination of Buddhism and traditional national religions, two that are mainly Islamic, and two (Hong Kong and Singapore) that, in the author's opinion, defy easy classification.

Colonial influences have also been varied. Eleven of the 14 countries have been exposed to colonial influences that have left distinct marks on economic and other social practices — China, Japan, and Thailand being the exceptions. All the developed countries except Japan bear the imprint of British institutions, as do three of the Asian economies — Malaysia, Singapore, and Hong Kong. The Philippines might be a fourth, but it is better described as a society with a strong U.S. veneer over a unique Malay-Spanish social mix. Brunei and most of the Pacific island states have also been British or U.S. colonies. The twentieth-century colonization of Korea and Taiwan by

Japan has also left important influences, as has the longer period of Dutch colonial government on Indonesia.

The region's political systems defy simple classification. Of the 14 countries, four — Japan, Canada, Australia, and New Zealand — are clearly parliamentary democracies associated with constitutional monarchy. Two — the United States and the Philippines — are presidential-congressional systems. Apart from the remaining colony (Hong Kong), most of the others have representative institutions combined with strong presidencies; in most, however, single-party dominance prevails. Those with the most significant opposition forces are Malaysia and Thailand. Opposition influences are also growing in South Korea and Taiwan. Centralized political power is greatest in China.[2]

In the face of such economic and social diversity, we now turn to evidence of concerted activity by both private interests and governments in the Pacific. The first phenomenon to address is the shifting world context in which Pacific development must take place. Subsequent chapters explore the following questions:

- In what sense, if any, is the Pacific a region with any definable unity or common cause?
- What Pacific regional "institutions" are being developed, and what role can they be expected to play?
- How will the Pacific countries link their regional interests and activities with global institutions, problems, and priorities for the future?
- What are Canada's interests in the region, and how can they be served by this country's participation in Pacific cooperative ventures?

---

2 See Robert Scalopino et al., *Regional Dynamics* (Jakarta: Centre for Strategic and International Studies, 1988), chap. 2.

## A Shifting World Economic Context

Regional identity in the Pacific rests in part on the changing character of international economic and political relations. Changing political perceptions, and slowly shifting political priorities and strategies, are interacting with economic changes. The economic growth of Western Europe and Japan since 1960 has reduced the *relative* competitiveness and economic power of both military "superpowers". Their shifting strategies, especially that of Gorbachev's Soviet Union, are driven by an awareness that their economic strength has been handicapped by the allocation of so many resources to military expenditures. Collective and efficient security for the future will likely mean that the Soviet Union and the United States will cooperate in reducing the waste of the arms race and in establishing an environment in which military adventurism — such as Iraq's — is discouraged and, if necessary, policed.

Accompanying this general shift to a multipolar world has been a shift in national strategies toward the reduction or removal of conventional economic intervention. This deregulation reflects, in part, the recognition that international competition is both inevitable and superior to national systems for regulating the allocation of resources and picking industrial winners. The Labour governments of Australia and New Zealand, for example, have been at least as active in their policy shifts as the more conservative governments of Canada and the United States. Policies to promote market-based trade and adjustment occupy a central role in most Pacific countries.

At the same time, however, intervention is taking new forms, most of them international: macroeconomic policy coordination, joint policies for the "sustainable development" of natural resources, other environmental policies, coordination of transport and communication systems, and integrated and more uniformly high-quality information systems. With growing evidence that even the largest economy in the world — the United States — is unable to sustain macroeconomic policies that differ significantly from those of its main trading partners, international policy coordination becomes even more important and national policies must become primarily adaptive. Similarly, environmental problems such as the destruction of the ozone layer and greenhouse effects cannot be addressed effectively without concerted international actions.

In the light of these shifts, Canada is challenged to examine two vital questions: to what extent do its domestic policies constrain its ability to compete internationally, and to what extent can its national interests be served by participating in Pacific initiatives and alliances in a constructive way?

One might tentatively conclude that international alliances affecting basic economic relationships are becoming more general but also technically more complex. This imposes a heavy burden on global institutions. It is evident that institutions in which as many as 160 national governments might be represented are likely to find consensus difficult to achieve. How important is a general consensus? Can smaller groups of countries, defined regionally or functionally, agree to deal with problems that need not concern the whole world? If they do tackle problems of world interest, can such groups provide the kind of leadership that other members of the international community might welcome? In some areas — macroeconomic policy coordination, for example — the high-income countries, such as the Group of Seven, can collectively provide much stability to the rest of the global economy. Regional trade arrangements, often comprehensive in character, coexist with multilateral regimes such as the GATT, and are accepted by the latter if they satisfy the provisions of GATT Article XXIV. In other areas — in particular, commodities — better information flows among major exporting and importing countries can assure greater dependability of both supplies and the rate of development. Among environmental issues, the sustainable development of renewable resources may require, first and foremost, the collaboration of major producers and consumers, but global solutions are likely to be essential in such cases as the greenhouse effect and ozone depletion.

## What Is the Pacific Region?

There is no simple definition of the Pacific region. Its most obvious feature is its geographical vastness. The 80th degree of west longitude is close to the west coast of South America, while the 100th degree of east longitude passes through Sumatra and western Thailand. It takes longer to fly from Vancouver to Hong Kong than it does to reach London, and both Canadian and U.S. capitals are almost twice as far from Tokyo as from London or Brussels. Sydney and Vancouver are both almost 5,000 miles from Tokyo, and the two Australian and Canadian cities are more than 7,500 miles apart. Although the ocean is a bridge as well as a barrier, much remains to be done to improve the efficiency of transportation and even of communications in the region. Are geographical dispersion and cultural diversity significant obstacles to economic cooperation?

The true identity of any region must be sought in a community of attitudes and interests. This was the fundamental reason for the creation of the Organisation for European Economic Co-operation and later the European Community. The evidence of the development of common interests in the Pacific is growing, notably in the western part of that region. One may observe that the international priorities of most Western Pacific countries focus on relations with their neighbors and on a conviction that a Western Pacific "prosperity sphere" that may well continue as the world's most economically vigorous zone. Trade-oriented development strategy, now growing in popularity elsewhere, has been exemplified by Japan since the 1960s and by the NIEs of the Western Pacific since the 1970s.

The Western Pacific zone is at present the north-south axis of the Pacific. As relations between North and South become an increasing challenge to international stability, a region such as the Western Pacific, which can exemplify constructive cooperation between countries at different stages of development, may make a unique contribution to meeting this challenge. This will be all the more so if China's economy can become responsive to market forces.

The Western Pacific is made up of three countries that are members of the Organisation for Economic Co-operation and Development (OECD): Japan, Australia, and New Zealand; the NIEs of South Korea, Taiwan, and Hong Kong; China; and the Association of Southeast Asian Nations (ASEAN) — Indonesia, Malaysia, the Philippines, Singapore, Thailand, and, since 1985, Brunei. There are also about 20 Pacific island states, including nine that are fully independent. These have a population of about 5 million, over 80 percent of which is in Papua-New Guinea and Fiji.

The North American economies — the United States and Canada — linked with the Pacific are currently the region's largest and third largest in terms of GNP (see Table 1). The vital relationship between the United States and Japan can benefit from the participation of the region's other countries, which can point out ways these two economic giants can jointly support the development of all economies in the region, rather than to dwell only on their own rivalry.

In this context, Canada, as the largest middle power in economic terms in the region and partner of the United States in the North American free trade arrangement, has a particular opportunity to provide a reconciling leadership — not merely as a third party, but as interpreter of the interests of the other major groups of countries in the Western Pacific. As members of the Organization of American States (OAS), Canada and the United States also have an opportunity to encourage the translation of Western Pacific trade-based strategies to major Latin American countries. This applies especially to Latin American countries that have been pressing for a larger role in Pacific institutions.

The cultural issue is an interesting one. There is no doubt that most Canadians would consider the cultures of Japan, China, and Southeast Asia as exotic, relative to Western Europe. In economic terms, a case can readily be made that the ingredients of commercial communication are highly favorable in the region. For example, there is no doubt that English is the accepted vehicle of business and economic communication in the Pacific. At no meeting of the various Pacific economic and trade conferences has there been any challenge to the legitimacy of the English language as the medium of communication, and only rarely has simultaneous translation been available. This does not relieve those who deal with East Asia of an obligation to probe the cultural basis of economic and business attitudes; it does make it easier for them to do so.

Western Pacific countries are, with one or two exceptions, active members of two multilateral organizations with a regional focus: the United Nations Economic and Social Commission for Asia and Pacific (ESCAP) and the Asian Development Bank. While both of these organizations focus on the Asia-Pacific region, they also include nine countries of South Asia westward to Afghanistan, the South Pacific island states, and the countries of the Western Pacific that are associated with the Soviet bloc. Canada and the United States are not included except as suppliers of capital to the Asian Development Bank.

## The Emergence of Pacific Institutions

Until November 1989, there were no institutions representing only the governments of countries around the Pacific Rim. One institution — the Pacific Economic Cooperation Conference (PECC) — includes public officials who are deemed to be "acting in a private capacity," but it also includes members of the business and academic-professional communities. Within PECC, each member is expected to have a committee — normally appointed by the government — that contains representatives from all three groups. Most of the business persons active in PECC are also associated with the Pacific Basin Economic Council (PBEC), while many of the academics involved are also members of the Pacific Trade and Development Conference (PAFTAD). Both of these groups have existed for over 20 years, while PECC held its first meeting in Canberra in 1980. Since then, it has held six further meetings: Bangkok (1982), Bali (1983), Seoul (1985), Vancouver (1986), Osaka (1988), and Auckland (November 1989). The next meeting is scheduled for Singapore in 1991.

Canada, the United States, and the 12 countries of East and Southeast Asia are all members of PECC. More loosely associated are the Pacific island states — nine are fully independent, seven others are in "free association" with "metropolitan countries", while seven others are dependencies. The only Western Pacific countries that currently have no formal connection with PECC are the Soviet Union and four other centrally planned states — North Korea, Vietnam, Cambodia, and Laos. The fact that the Soviet Union is pressing its claims for membership ultimately could lead to universal Western Pacific participation, but the degree of regional consensus that would then be possible is still a matter of some doubt.

Until September 1990, only Canada and the United States among the countries of the Eastern Pacific were full members of PECC. The strong linkages between Japan and the United States, which together account for about 80 percent of the GDP of PECC members, make the North American presence both significant and inevitable. The attraction of the North American market and the importance of the United States to Japan's security have guaranteed transPacific relations the highest priority in the national policies of these two economic leaders. Should the Japanese take increasing responsibility for their own defense, and should North-South relations in the Korean peninsula become less confrontational, priorities in trans-Pacific relations will become more economic in focus. Such trends will, however, depend greatly on the prospects for Mikhail Gorbachev's initiatives. Certainly, the possibility of Soviet participation in PECC ultimately will be governed by judgments about the contribution to the new detente that such participation could foster. Policymakers must be torn between the higher profile role that PECC would achieve if both the United States and the Soviet Union were members, and the concern that consensual positions on economic matters might prove more difficult to achieve and less important than the dance of detente that might easily displace the consensus-planning activity of economic conferences. Any discussion of Soviet membership in PECC must include mention of Japanese opposition, based in no small degree on the continued Soviet occupation of four small islands north of Hokkaido that it seized near the end of World War II. Security and other (including symbolic) political considerations predominate, but it is the judgment of political observers in Japan and elsewhere that no other significant factor obstructs Japanese cooperation with Gorbachev's Soviet Union.

PECC's other central membership issue is the role of the Latin American states. Three of these — Mexico, Peru, and Chile — have shown substantial interest in joining for some time and, over the past two years, have made formal applications for membership. These applications were accepted at a meeting of the PECC Standing Committee in September 1990. These countries have been active observers of PECC meetings for several years and have participated in interconference task force meetings, especially on fisheries, minerals, and energy and trade issues. Although Latin America's international interests have focused on Western Hemisphere links through the OAS, the Inter-American Development Bank, and regional economic trade groups or associations, there is growing interest in both global and transPacific economic relations. This has been reflected in such developments as Mexico's recent membership in the GATT and Japan's increasing importance as a source of new technology and capital for Latin America. Not unimportant is that NIEs and developing countries on both sides of the ocean see transPacific relations as a counterweight to their sometimes uncomfortable associations with the superpower in their region. U.S and Japanese statesmen, moreover, are aware that sharing their regional hegemonic roles can contribute to smoother and less risky transPacific economic relations.

Hong Kong's application for membership in PECC was also accepted in September 1990. The reason for the delay in this case was unrelated, however, to any hesitancy on the part of PECC members. This means that there are now 18 members, plus the Pacific island group delegation.

## Asia Pacific Economic Cooperation

In January 1989, Prime Minister Robert Hawke of Australia initiated a process that ultimately resulted in the creation of the first modest Pacific Rim institution that was truly intergovernmental in nature. At its first meeting — in Canberra in November 1989 — the new body was given the acronym APEC, signifying Asia Pacific Economic Cooperation. No organizational title was included, so it was described as a "ministerial-level meeting." Twelve nations were represented by one to three ministers each. The United States sent a very strong delegation that included three with cabinet rank: the secretaries of State and Commerce, and the U.S. Trade Representative. Japan was represented by its Foreign Minister and the Minister of International Trade and Industry (MITI). Minister of International Trade John Crosbie represented Canada. Many of the other countries were also represented by their foreign minister and senior economic minister (only Canada, Australia, and New Zealand have combined ministries).

Several issues arose during the period leading up to the November 1989 meeting:

- What governments would be included?
- What future organizational evolution and policy priorities would be likely to emerge from APEC?
- What major issues would likely affect APEC's future prospects and structure?

The decision on the list of invitees caused some conflict. It appeared at first that the Australians had in mind a Western Pacific group only, which would have excluded Canada and the United States. This reflected a division that has existed before in Australian government opinion. A number of considerations appeared to support this option in 1989. Among these was the division of opinion in the Japanese government, with *some* MITI officials being inclined toward a Western Pacific grouping. There has also been much agitation in some of the NIEs and developing countries — including South Korea, China, Singapore, and Thailand — over the U.S. government's unilateral pressure on such issues as the access to their markets for U.S. financial services and their failure to adopt strong legislation to protect intellectual property following the U.S. model. This opposition was ultimately not so strong, however, as to exclude the United States and Canada, which left no doubt that they expected to be there.

A more serious problem arose with respect to the presence of China, Taiwan, and Hong Kong. For political reasons, China could not accept representation from what it views as its province of Taiwan at a purely governmental meeting. And in the aftermath of the events in Tiananmen Square in June 1989, there was some reluctance on the part of some countries to encourage Chinese participation. In the end, neither China nor Taiwan was represented at the November meeting, and Hong Kong's participation was not pressed. In the latter half of 1989, the case was frequently made that all administrative entities that represented separate customs and trade policy units had a legitimate role in international economic cooperation organizations. Since Hong Kong is a member of the GATT, and since

China has agreed to its continuing to have separate membership beyond 1997, Hong Kong has a strong case for its separate representation in APEC as well as in PECC. China has not rejected the possibility that Taiwan could also achieve a separate role in the GATT, but it has insisted that this cannot be supported until China's own status in the GATT has been established. There is a further ambiguity associated with the fact that APEC is not purely a group of trade ministers but includes foreign ministers as well.

The relationship between PECC and APEC reflects this last issue, since PECC includes both China and Taiwan — or Chinese Taipei, to use the official PECC name — while it may be some time before both are active in APEC. Mexico, Chile, Peru, and even the Soviet Union will find it easier to join the lesser tripartite PECC than the governmental APEC.

Resistance on grounds of national or subregional interests is likely to continue. Japan, for example, will probably remain reluctant to accept the Soviet Union's joining both PECC and APEC until its northern territories are restored. The governments of the ASEAN countries may continue to resist Latin American membership in APEC, as this would dilute their leading role among developing countries in the region. Their attitude toward membership for the Soviet Union and China remains unclear, and could be linked to the basis for decisions on China, Taiwan, and Hong Kong.

APEC members are also anxious that the group's size or diversity of interests should not be so great as to make it ineffectual. In some cases, notably among the ASEAN countries, there appears to be resistance to Chinese and Latin American participation on grounds of competition — both direct economic competition in the trade of labor-intensive manufactures and competition in political influence in the region, especially from other major developing countries. For this reason, ASEAN's more political ministers have favored building APEC on the foundation of the ASEAN dialogue with its Pacific partners. This approach has only recently found scope for South Korean involvement in that dialogue and probably would have difficulty in accommodating the large Latin American countries. One of the major contributions that the Pacific countries could make to global economic cooperation is their potential to propose consensual North-South positions on multilateral negotiations. Accordingly, the wider participation of the region's developing countries in APEC could be of crucial importance.

Content, however, must be present. APEC's first meeting indicated that the participants' priorities were an improved database for macroeconomic forecasting, the development of sufficient consensus among trade ministers on the issues in multilateral trade negotiations so that the regional group might contribute to a successful outcome, and agreement on policies affecting sustainable development of the Pacific fisheries.[3] All of these argue for a broader APEC membership. Quality improvement in macroeconomic data, for example, would be of particular value to the region's developing countries, which should gain from technology transfer and other aid to that end.

The APEC initiative toward consensus positions by member countries in the Uruguay Round of GATT negotiations is the single most important activity of APEC's first year. At the November 1989 meeting, two meetings of APEC trade ministers were scheduled for 1990: for September in Vancouver and for December in Brussels, just prior to the Uruguay Round's final negotiating sessions. The first of these meetings took place on September 11–12. The second meeting did not take place.

The Pacific group is representative of all the interests affecting key issues in the GATT negotiations, including agri-

---

3 The statements released by the ministers after their first meeting are reproduced in H.E. English, ed., *Pacific Initiatives in Global Trade* (Halifax: Institute for Research on Public Policy, 1990), Appendix III. See also "Asia-Pacific Community," *Far Eastern Economic Review*, November 16, 1989, pp. 10–19.

culture (tropical and temperate), textiles, services, intellectual property, and safeguards and other GATT rules. Both the developing and the developed countries have a stake in expanding the scope and effectiveness of the multilateral trading system. Any consensus position they can work out that encompasses these issues would be attractive to all but the most reluctant GATT participants. In particular, other developing countries would welcome the success of such efforts, since their role in the GATT to date has not matched in influence that of the Pacific developing countries in PECC and APEC.

There are many issues in the current round of GATT negotiations that will require follow-up negotiations on a multilateral basis or regionally in 1991 and beyond. Some of these have an important Pacific focus. Among these are the specific procedures related to phasing out of textile production under the Multi-Fibre Arrangement (MFA); the application of any service trade framework to sectors of priority interest to the region; the strengthening of constraints on the use of antidumping and countervailing duties and other practices that are applied in excessively protectionist ways; and a regime for harmonizing investment regulations. The basis for membership in the multilateral trade regime for countries such as China and Taiwan will have a direct relevance to other Pacific trading partners.

The Pacific fisheries issues on the APEC agenda have been anticipated by the fisheries task force of PECC. They include cooperation among the developing countries of the South Pacific, transfer of technology in this sector, and, more recently, an interest in controlling drift-net fishing. One of the notable features of fisheries cooperation has been the particularly active involvement of Peru, Chile, and other Latin American "observers". Peru has hosted meetings on this issue, and PECC's work in this area has helped to reinforce the efforts of those Latin American countries to join PECC.

## How Will APEC Evolve?

It has been suggested that PECC and APEC activity might lead
to the establishment of a Pacific OECD. Scholarly work on this
topic has usually labelled this OPTAD, or Organization for
Pacific Trade and Development.[4] The concept reflects the belief
that the importance of North-South cooperation as a meeting
of equals is the order of the day for the future, but that the
OECD itself is too much a creature of the rich. The notion of
extending OECD membership to the NIEs as they "graduate"
from the development phase is potentially divisive from the
point of view of many developing countries; in a Pacific context,
it would discriminate among ASEAN members in particular.

On the other hand, an OPTAD could emulate the OECD in
a number of respects, and could be a kind of partner institution. Like the OECD, it would probably be based largely on
policy research, development, and consultation. By strengthening the information system, it should put all discussion
among its members on a more common foundation for policy
harmonization and negotiation. By strengthening research
capacity related to priority policy issues, it would greatly assist
the development of policy innovation internationally and na-
tionally, especially through support for networking among
research institutions in the developing countries and between
them and the more established institutions in the developed
countries.

The question of how large a secretariat is required for such
activities is an important one. The immediate answer of those
associated with APEC is that it should be small for some time
to come. So far, APEC has avoided giving any priority to
"institutionalization". It has depended on the *ad hoc* efforts of
the various national bureaucracies, and it has also relied on

---

4 For early appraisal of this idea, see Peter Drysdale, "The Proposal for an
  Organization for Pacific Trade and Development Revisited," *Asian Survey*
  (December 1983).

the work of PECC and its task forces and forums. These, in turn, have depended almost entirely on private research institutions, and universities, in some cases benefiting from public funds. It has been a lean process, but quite effective in those areas of direct interest to APEC's initial agenda.

This rather mundane discussion of procedures relates to a more basic conceptual debate. In the past several decades, the question of what principles should govern regional cooperation has focused almost entirely on the theory of economic integration. This rests on neoclassical trade theory and its application primarily to European economic integration. It has now been applied in the North American context to the Canada-U.S. Free Trade Agreement (FTA). Basically, it implies — though this has seldom been all that explicit — that nations have a choice between various levels of integration, which include at least four main categories:

- *a free trade area*, where member countries are committed to free trade between them but retain separate commercial policies with respect to nonmembers;
- *a customs union*, where members agree to adopt a common commercial policy with respect to nonmembers;
- *a common market*, where members agree to freedom not only of trade but also of movement of factors such as labor and capital; and
- *an economic union*, where members agree to adopt common economic policy and even common public tax and expenditure policies.

The choice among these categories can vary widely, depending on the interest of participants. Two examples will illustrate this. In Europe in the 1950s, the original six members of the Community agreed to move toward a high level of integration — basically, a common market. More recently, they have become committed to a more complete common market and a partial economic union — in particular, a monetary union. The Canada-U.S. FTA, by contrast, is basically a more modest free trade area with some elements of a common market, since there is provision for freer movement of capital between the two countries.

The main reason for the difference between the European and North American schemes for economic integration is political. The Europeans have come close to adopting the concept of a United States of Europe because they have few reservations about giving up a large amount of their economic sovereignty. This is mainly because they see political benefits in terms of added strength, and few significant economic or social costs. Moreover, they remember vividly the costs of nationalism in Europe in this century. There are also many states in the European Community, so that no single one can be dominant.

In the Canada-U.S. case, the Canadian view is that the costs of loss of sovereignty are greater in a two-member regional group in which one is very much larger than the other. Furthermore, it can be argued that most of the benefits of economic integration can be achieved through a free trade area, and that there are more social costs in moving to a closer form of integration.

These differences are probably greater if one considers an integration scheme among developing countries. This may be because, almost by definition, such countries believe that their infrastructure differences require more public intervention, and that their industries require infant-industry protection. This attitude is reinforced if the members of a group of developing countries differ in size or degree of development, but it may also be the result of uncertainty about just where their economic potentials are greater.

A still greater problem may exist where an integration scheme involves both developed and developing countries. The former may be much more willing to participate, especially in stronger sectors and in the movement of capital; the latter may well feel, for reasons already cited, that they are at a more general disadvantage, even in the processing of natural resources and in labor-intensive activity. A rather unusual test of the possibilities for free trade between countries with marked differences in wage and development levels exists in the proposed U.S.-Mexico FTA.

For large groups of countries at different development levels, a neoclassical free trade arrangement or integration scheme seems most improbable. This is why a new concept of regionalism is probably necessary and, in fact, may be emerging in a pragmatic form in the Pacific. Such countries may agree that trade liberalization is desirable as an engine of growth and a discipline to reduce inefficiencies in the economy. At the same time, they see cooperation as a means of dealing collectively with development problems. This will include several of the following elements:

- reduction of tariff and nontariff barriers affecting goods and services most likely to become leading export sectors for developing countries, and avoidance of excessive protection by developing countries against products or services likely to be supplied more efficiently by developed countries;
- developmentally sound foreign investment to support those sectors with potential export strength, and investment and official aid for skills development, technology adaptation, and other infrastructural improvements;
- macroeconomic policy coordination and development of the informational base for a common approach to problems of market imperfections, including gaps in financial markets and sustainable development in the resource sectors.

The countries of the Pacific region are moving in directions that are compatible with such guidelines. The scope for regional cooperation and issue-specific alliances in these matters seems substantial.

# 2

# Pacific Economic
# Priorities in the 1990s

The agenda of issues being discussed in the context of the Pacific Economic Cooperation Conference (PECC) and in other regional institutions includes trade and related investment policies, the Pacific macroeconomic outlook and related policy coordination, natural resource development and market conditions, and science and technology — including technology transfer. This chapter concentrates on the first two, and briefly addresses the others.

## Trade Policy Cooperation in the Uruguay Round and Beyond

The Pacific region has a vital role to play in the multilateral trading system, and its interest in the current, Uruguay Round of negotiations under the General Agreement on Tariffs and Trade (GATT) is very high. Two aspects of trade policies in the region warrant review: direct cooperation in the Uruguay Round, and cooperation on a larger regional basis as a complement and stimulus to the multilateral process.

In both contexts, the Pacific countries will continue to act mainly through national negotiators, but also in groups — for example, the Association of Southeast Asian Nations (ASEAN) have consulted and acted together, notably in the early stages of the Uruguay Round, while the Cairns Group, the majority of whose members are on the Pacific Rim, [1] is taking a leading role in GATT efforts to reduce agricultural protectionism. In some cases, U.S. and Canadian negotiating positions in the Round have tended to converge as a result of bilateral agreement in areas of common interest, as part of their negotiations on the Canada-U.S. Free Trade Agreement (FTA).

The Pacific Rim countries reflect as wide a variety of trade policy interests as any grouping of countries. The United States seeks to remain active as exporter of certain resource (especially agricultural) products, technology-intensive manufactures, and services. Japan concentrates on maintaining its spectacular performance in manufactured products and, more recently, in services. Canada, Australia, and New Zealand continue to export resource-based products, and are also seeking more manufacturing and service export "niches".

The newly industrialized economies (NIEs) — South Korea, Taiwan, Hong Kong, and Singapore — which began to grow as suppliers of labor-intensive goods, have increasingly diversified their exports of manufactured goods. Some have also established credentials as producers and traders of services, notably in construction, airlines, tourism, and, in Hong Kong's case, specialized financial and commercial services.

Singapore's economy is even more service-based than Hong Kong's, but the traditional strength of the other five ASEAN

---

1 The 14 members of the Cairns Group are Argentina, Australia, Brazil, Canada, Chile, Colombia, Fiji, Hungary, Indonesia, Malaysia, New Zealand, the Philippines, Thailand, and Uruguay. Of the 11 Pacific Rim countries, only Chile and Colombia are not currently members of PECC, although Chile has actively sought membership for several years, and formally joins PECC in May 1991.

countries lies in a variety of resource-based sectors, many of them tropical — rubber, palm and coconut products, rice, cane sugar, tropical fruit, hardwoods, and so on. Most of these countries, however, also have a growing capacity and interest in exporting both resource-based and labor-intensive manufactures. Tourism and air transport services are also significant "export" sectors.

China is a potentially formidable competitor for these countries. It is seen as a center of rapid growth, provided that its emergence as a producer of manufactures continues to evolve out of its "open door" policy and a related increased scope for private enterprise and joint ventures. Its manufactured exports are likely to concentrate on the labor-intensive sectors, and may soon present a formidable challenge to the ASEAN group's ambition to develop similar exports.

The only other group of countries whose interest in Pacific-basin trade is clearly established comprises the Pacific island states and dependencies. With only a few exceptions — Papua-New Guinea in copper, gold, and oil, and Nauru in phosphates — these small and specialized economies have a preponderant interest in fisheries, tree crops, sugar cane, and tourism.

Most of the high-priority issues being negotiated in the Uruguay Round are of interest to one or more groups of these Pacific countries. Should the Round prove successful, trade levels throughout the region will be enhanced considerably. The Pacific countries understand this well enough, and are pushing hard for success. While there are grounds for optimism, prospects for success are far from certain given the participation of other GATT parties less committed to the Pacific's full range of trade liberalization priorities, or at least less urgently so. Accordingly, purely regional initiatives are likely to receive a high priority after the Uruguay Round concludes.

A selection of the major trade issues and their meaning for the GATT's Pacific players is thus in order. These issues are:

agriculture and tropical products; traditional, relatively labor-intensive manufactures; technology-intensive goods and services and related "new issues" — trade-related intellectual property and investment measures; and strengthening of the rules, institutional structure, and practices of the GATT. If the Pacific countries can spell out the bases of their trade-liberalizing positions on these matters, the region's importance in the overall GATT framework could lead to these positions being adopted in the wider multilateral context, either during the Uruguay Round or by subsequent initiatives.

## Agriculture and Tropical Products

Agriculture and tropical products constitute an almost ideal first example. Action to liberalize trade in agricultural products is long overdue. The GATT has been a near failure in this sector because of the commitment of so many countries to protectionism. It is ironic that the United States, one of the strongest agricultural producers, was primarily responsible for the virtual exclusion of agriculture from the GATT negotiations in the early years of the agreement's application. Only now has the enormous cost in terms of higher food prices and inefficient international allocation of agricultural production become so apparent that countries have reconsidered their entrenched protectionism.

In 1985, the United States decided to put in place additional ammunition for the bargaining battle by introducing "fighting" export subsidies to meet those of other major trading countries, especially those of the European Community (EC). Meanwhile, other countries, led by Australia, established the Cairns Group — a "ginger" group within the GATT wishing to take aim at export subsidies granted countries whose domestic agricultural policies create such surpluses that they cannot otherwise be absorbed in world markets. The Cairns Group has collectively prepared negotiating positions reflecting the interests of its members as exporters with some comparative advantages.[2] It is worth noting, however, that in some sectors, the policies of some members are inconsistent with the principles of free trade that the group espouses. Canada, for example, maintains supply-management policies that substantially increase prices in certain sectors and that require import controls to achieve their aims.[3]

Within the broader context of PECC, the same issues have been addressed in a Trade Policy Forum and in another group known as the Agricultural Policy, Trade and Development Task Force. This latter group sponsored the preparation and discussion of studies assessing the cost to individual countries of their high-cost food production arising out of price-support and supply-management policies. The effect was to urge the Pacific countries to examine their comparative advantages in various agricultural sectors and to explore the possibility of shifting their pattern of agricultural activity to products that require less protection.

These efforts contributed to an attitude of compromise in the Trade Policy Forum, which endeavored to relate agricultural protection to other trade policy issues. For example, the aims of tropical developing countries to achieve free entry into temperate-zone developed countries for their agricultural, fishery, and forest products could be enhanced if those developing

---

2 See the excellent article by William M. Miner, "Negotiating Agriculture," in Murray G. Smith, ed., *Canada, The Pacific, and Global Trade* (Halifax: Institute for Research on Public Policy, 1989).

3 A recent report calling attention to this inconsistency estimates that if Canada were to eliminate its support systems — mainly concentrated in the dairy, poultry and eggs, and grain sectors — farm output would drop by one-sixth. It also estimates that each job saved by support systems costs an average of $100,000 (see Organisation for Economic Co-operation and Development, "Economy-Wide Effects of Agricultural Policies in OECD Countries," *OECD Economic Studies* 13 [Winter 1989–1990]). Even if one disputes the net effect, especially of the grain supports which adversely affect meat production in the same region, policy rationalization is clearly overdue.

countries could agree to remove or reduce subsidies and other protective activity affecting products in the livestock and feed grains group and in the red meats group, where comparative advantages generally favor the temperate-zone and land-rich countries.

Both groups of countries can benefit from the mutual exchange of processed natural products. However, there are two qualifications handicapping complete reciprocity in such products. First, processing sectors in developing countries may have a legitimate claim to infant-industry protection, especially since their ability to develop processing activity has long been limited by escalated tariffs or nontariff barriers affecting the import of processed products into developed (as well as other developing) countries. Second, the developed countries made an early commitment to reduce and, in most cases, to eliminate barriers on tropical products without reciprocity. Were they now to demand that these concessions be tied to reciprocal concessions by the developing countries, this could be represented as a retreat from that commitment.

One way to satisfy the perception of a new commitment by the two groups to trade liberalization would be for the developing countries to open up their markets to natural products from the developed countries as a *quid pro quo* for better access to developed countries for their labor-intensive manufactures, including textile products.

## Traditional Manufactures

Traditional manufactures — textiles, steel, automobiles, for example — were the cornerstone of nonresource-based secondary industry in the advanced industrial countries, and are the first to be manufactured in many of the developing countries. They are not a homogeneous group in other important respects, however, as we shall see.

## Textiles

Unlike steel and automobiles, the textile industry — clothing production, in particular — is clearly the most labor intensive. Primary textile production is actually quite capital intensive. At one time, Canada's main concern was whether it could match U.S. plants in economies of scale in the production of yarn and cloth. Compared with U.S. or British plants, Canadian plants could not achieve volume in particular runs of cloth and so could not efficiently use textile machines. The "frequent changeovers" problem was as characteristic of this sector as it was of automobile assembly plants of the 1950s, and it is also characteristic of many smaller protected economies.

Historically, clothing production — as opposed to primary textiles — was often a home or cottage industry, and it was not thought necessary to protect it. During the past 50 years, however, the emphasis has changed. The manufacture of clothing and other textile products has become basic to many industrializing economies — first Japan, Hong Kong, South Korea, and Taiwan, and now Southeast and South Asia, as well as some Latin American countries.

At first, these countries imported their primary textiles and, later, the machinery to produce them — thus providing the inputs to their clothing industry. Primary textiles have remained relatively competitive in the larger developed countries because of their low labor component, but the labor intensiveness of clothing production has given the more advanced developing countries a clear advantage in that standard range of clothing products.

This situation has generated concern and calls for protection by the primary textile producers of developed countries, which were reluctant to see the domestic clothing sectors undermined. Although they could, if their machinery were reasonably up to date and management were capable, export primary textiles even to low-labor-cost countries where the clothing industries were stronger, they were reluctant to lose a captured domestic market to which they enjoyed an assured access. At first, the clothing industries cooperated in the campaign for maintained protection, but firms finally came to realize that they could be lower-cost producers if they imported their primary textiles and concentrated on fashion goods. In these sectors, they could respond more quickly to changes in market demand than could the larger-volume producers of more standardized clothing items in Asia.

The Canada-U.S. free trade negotiations reflected these shifting views. Some Canadian apparel manufacturers were interested in using imported primary products from Asia, as these could reduce costs and increase scope for export to the United States. Primary producers in the United States put pressure on their Canadian counterparts to resist those aspects of the agreement that might enable Canadian clothing producers to exploit that strategy. The U.S. producers of both primary and downstream products now seem to be hanging on to their domestic markets, and have succeeded in keeping the U.S. government from living up to its commitments under the international Multi-Fibre Arrangement (MFA).[4] However, it must be acknowledged that other signatories to that agreement, including Canada, have done little better.

Meanwhile, developing countries are also divided on these issues. The NIEs, in particular — the main source of traded textile products — have quotas and import-growth commitments that permit them to retain the bulk of the presently available market. Without these quotas favoring established suppliers, the new lower-wage suppliers of such products — Thailand and China, for example — would acquire larger

---

4 The MFA, which has existed for nearly three decades in one form or another, permits the use of bilateral quotas in exchange for commitments to increase imports by a modest percentage each year. This results in rigidity in production conditions and makes it particularly difficult for new producing countries to gain a foothold in this market. Established suppliers control quota distribution.

market shares. While the NIEs are gradually shifting out of the product lines most likely to be supplied more competitively by others, they are reluctant to give up the quotas on which their present level of exports depends. So there sometimes seems to be little commitment to reform on the part of these countries.

There have been calls for a phasing out of the MFA over a five-to-ten-year period, as a part of the Uruguay Round package of concessions.[5] Whether or not this occurs, a regional initiative — by, say, the five most developed Pacific economies — could represent a commitment to a more rational treatment of textiles trade. Under such an initiative, these countries might increase their import quotas each year until, by later in the 1990s, the MFA and other quantitative restrictions would cease to apply, and by 2000 at the latest, tariff-only treatment could be achieved. They might also agree on higher growth rates for imports from countries with below-average shares of world markets in a specified recent year. The parallel with guidelines suggested by some developed countries for reducing agricultural protection is not purely coincidental.

## Steel

The relationship between primary steel — a highly capital-intensive manufacturing sector — and the iron and steel products business is similar to that between primary textiles and clothing, in the sense that many downstream products are produced under much less capital-intensive technological conditions. In terms of comparative advantages based on factor endowments, one might expect to find this industry concentrated in high-wage countries — especially those with ready access to supplies of iron ore, steel scrap, and metallurgical and thermal coal and other applicable energy sources. Thus,

---

5 See, for example, Ippei Yamazawa, "The Textile Trade Issue in the Uruguay Round Negotiations," in H.E. English, ed., *Pacific Initiatives in Global Trade* (Halifax: Institute for Research on Public Policy, 1990), pp. 127–136.

the United States and Canada should rank high as producers and net exporters of basic steel, while downstream products should be manufactured in countries with lower wage costs. The relatively high "weight-for-value" characteristics of basic steel, however, make comparative advantage substantially less effective. Under normal conditions, the proportion of the trade of steel relative to its production is lower than for most products, and all countries with large domestic markets have, or try to have, their own primary steel.

This tendency has been accentuated by the wars of the twentieth century and by the consequent perceived need to have secure local supplies. After the post–1945 reconstruction period, the demand for steel leveled out, and the developed countries had less incentive to build new plants to serve their domestic markets. The markets of developing countries were not very large, so there was only a limited incentive to relocate mills to serve them. In the United States, in particular, where most steel production was located in the interior, close to raw materials and major domestic markets, the incentive to relocate seemed weak. Meanwhile, the Japanese located new, modern plants at deep-water ports, minimizing the cost disadvantages of relying on imported raw materials. The Europeans also rebuilt and modernized their steel industries.

After their reconstruction needs were satisfied, both the Europeans and the Japanese were in a position to supply overseas markets more conveniently and more efficiently than could most U.S. producers. Later, in the 1970s, the leveling out of world demand for steel and the substitution of other materials — partly as a result of higher energy prices — led many steel manufacturers in the developed countries to adopt "marginal-cost pricing".[6] Japanese companies, facing new compe-

---

6 Marginal-cost pricing refers to the practice of setting a price so as to cover only direct costs (labor, materials, energy, and so on) but little or no overhead (fixed plant amortization, for example). It is attractive to firms with excess capacity or older plants not valued at replacement cost.

tition from South Korean and East Asian newcomers, have used this practice to penetrate Asian markets, though it was not necessary to meet U.S. competition. Canadian producers found themselves to be competitive, at least relative to U.S. producers, because they had substantially expanded their plants in the 1940s and 1950s and were able to capture a larger share of the U.S. market for a range of products. Pressure from U.S. industry to use "orderly marketing", however, probably has kept Canadian producers from expanding their shares of the U.S. market beyond 3–5 percent.

All incursions by steel producers — including those from Canada — into foreign markets have been met by demands for protection, usually in the form of orderly marketing agreements and countervailing duties. The result has been a continuing protectionist conflict among national enterprises unwilling to adapt to changing international market conditions; each claims the right to reserve its traditional national market, and defends that "right" on the grounds that its rivals engage in unfair competitive practices. Only a more dynamic market can be counted on to break this log-jam. Two ways to contribute to reason here might be to identify, on a multilateral basis, the true sources of cost differences among countries that export steel, and to concur on appropriate measures for policing an agreed-on definition of unacceptable subsidies.

## Automobiles

The third "traditional" industry that illustrates the international competitiveness problem, particularly in the Pacific, is the automobile industry. Like the other sectors, it is a mixture of more and less labor-intensive subsectors. The assembly of automobiles employs much labor, relative to steel and even primary textiles, but differs in two important respects.

First, it is integrated with a complex set of component suppliers. Some are small scale and relatively labor intensive;

others produce complex components, such as body stampings and automotive transmissions, and are highly capital intensive. This has produced the challenge of how to manage effectively both component production and assembly through the best forms of access to suppliers, inventory control, and production flexibility in relation to shifts in market demand. The varying response to this challenge has been a feature of the competitive strategies of Japanese and U.S. automakers.

The other distinctive feature is the great importance to the auto industry of product differentiation and, therefore, of nonplant labor and management. This is manifest both in product design and quality control — and, hence, in research and development — and in marketing. The consequence of the centrality of these activities is that consumer brand loyalties became an important feature of rivalry among a relatively few leading firms, each seeking to secure and maintain much larger market shares than are required to maintain economies of plant size. Market shares in automobiles cannot be as readily recaptured using mainly cost and price competition as they can for most steel and textile products.

Since 1971, Japanese auto firms have become formidable international competitors. They have achieved this through the development of efficient production management, and of fuel-efficient cars in the wake of the oil price shocks of the 1970s.

Although Japanese producers' market share rose in the late 1970s, the 1979–80 hike in oil prices generated inflationary expectations that resulted in coordinated "tight money" policy among central bankers in the developed countries. This dampened demand for durables. At the same time, Japanese dependence on energy imports kept the value of the yen low. By the time oil prices began to fall in 1982, the U.S. government was experiencing a growing fiscal deficit — the result of tax reductions and increased defense spending. The effect of this, especially given a low U.S. savings rate, was to hold interest rates up through government borrowing, which attracted foreign capital inflow. The resulting high U.S. dollar encouraged imports and discouraged exports. This was significantly reflected in the automotive products trade, not only with Japan, but with Canada as well. The fall in oil and other commodity prices during this period helped keep the Canadian dollar low relative to the U.S. dollar.

All in all, Japanese automotive trade was distorted mainly by macroeconomic considerations, which also made it more difficult for U.S. auto producers to overcome the market-share positions the Japanese manufacturers had achieved in the 1970s. The quality and dependability record of their cars, repeatedly attested to in U.S. consumer publications, reinforced owner preferences. As for sales of U.S. cars to the Japanese market, although it is clear that both Japanese customers' attitudes and the distribution system continue to make penetration of that market very difficult, it is highly unlikely that these factors played a part at all comparable to the above considerations in restricting U.S. products to a very modest market share in Japan.

The only non-Japanese automotive producer in the Pacific that has achieved export success is Hyundai, of South Korea. Using a link with Mitsubishi that has mainly affected its engine design, this large company has made a substantial incursion into the North American market since 1985. Its success has been assisted by two trade factors. One is the voluntary export arrangement that the United States forced on Japanese automakers in 1981. This encouraged the Japanese to supply higher-priced models in order to maintain profits in the larger markups available on those models. It also created a shortage of cheaper models, which allowed Hyundai to step in and capture a significant market share. The other factor was the application of the generalized system of preferences to South Korean car exports.[7] In Canada, this has meant that the South

---

7 The generalized system of preferences (GSP) was promoted by the United Nations Conference on Trade and Development (UNCTAD). It was a scheme...

Koreans are able to avoid the 7.5 percent tariff charged on Japanese car imports; at times, this resulted in an almost equivalent price advantage for lower-priced Hyundai Ponys as compared with comparable Japanese models. Hyundai's market share has recently declined due to its dependability record falling somewhat short of that of Japanese cars. As a price-quality tradeoff, however, the Pony remains attractive.

From 1985 to 1987, the U.S. dollar lost nearly half its value relative to the Japanese yen, and from 1987 to 1989, the dollar depreciated 20–25 percent relative to the South Korean won. This depreciation, together with threats of protectionist legislation by the U.S. Congress, encouraged Japanese and South Korean automakers to invest in North America directly. Honda, Toyota, and Hyundai, for example, have all established plants in Canada. At the same time, U.S.-based companies have continued to develop joint ventures in automobile manufacture and trade. Small U.S. cars — such as the Dodge Colt — have been produced in Japan for North American companies for some time. Many new initiatives have accompanied the recent surge of Asian investment. Japanese producers are now shipping some of their models from North American plants back to Japan; the value of these exports is now comparable to Canada-U.S. trade in automobiles.

The future pattern of trade remains difficult to predict. It is clear, however, that adjustment to all the factors that have been cited here is now well advanced. U.S.-based producers, for example, have sought to adopt and adapt Japanese management and labor-management practices. Because of the traditional prestige of automobile companies in North America, intra-industry trade and investment deals will continue, and

---

7 - *cont'd.*

...by which developed countries were called upon to grant lower tariff rates on imports from developing countries. The major developed countries adopted this practice, but hedged by excluding sensitive sectors such as textiles or by setting quotas on the amounts to which the GSP would apply.

the diversity of production requirements in the manufacture of components and vehicles indicates a two-way trade to the fullest extent permitted by macroeconomic policy, trade policy, and "cultural" constraints. It seems unlikely that the manufacture of final products in the automobile sector will shift to East Asia quite as massively as was the case with consumer electronic goods, though component production and assembly may be distributed widely, and two-way trade in automotive products between North America and Asia will continue, probably with less formal government intervention than in the past.

## The Dynamics of Traditional Manufactures in the Pacific

So far, the discussion has centered largely on the developed countries and the Asian NIEs. What will be the role of the developing countries, especially the members of ASEAN, in investment and trade in traditional manufactures?

The appropriate pattern is clearest for textile products. The shift of production to the Southeast Asian countries has already begun. Economic logic would argue for the textile products — especially the clothing industries — to take the lead in this shift, while primary textiles would continue to be exported from the NIEs and China. For this to happen, however, the developed countries will have to open up their markets to foreign manufactures of clothing products, and the NIEs will have to abandon the quota-protected "established-growth" advantage they have over their lower-wage neighbors.

What of steel and automobiles? On the grounds of comparative advantage and resource endowment, steel production will be based in those countries with good access to the necessary raw materials, larger markets, and relatively more abundant capital than labor. They will then supply rolled steel to the domestic producers of products that are manufactured with more labor-intensive techniques.

It is not clear that South Korea's long-term advantage lies in primary iron and steel production. It is more likely that such production will occur in China and perhaps Indonesia, if energy sources suffice. Other developing countries will concentrate relatively more on "downstream" products and will need export market access for some of these in order to achieve scale economies.

All countries, it seems, want to produce automobiles. It is increasingly recognized, however, that to do so without imposing enormous costs on their economies, they must have well worked out arrangements with one or more major international automakers, which are able to locate component manufactures in a larger number of countries and major assembly units in those with the largest domestic markets. To achieve this, countries such as those in ASEAN will need to ensure the virtually free flow of components within their region and easy access for exports of the most capital-intensive and technology intensive components from the developed countries and NIEs.

The successful exploitation of these comparative advantages in the traditional manufacturing industries means that the developed countries will have to make their markets available to exporters of the most labor-intensive components and final products in the pattern — for example, clothing and iron and steel products. In return, they can hope to sell on more favorable terms the most technologically complex components of automobiles to assemblers that will operate in all of the larger markets. This leads to a discussion of the nontraditional manufactures and related services trade.

## Technology-Intensive Goods and Services

Technology-intensive goods and services, along with trade-related investment measures, constitute the "new issues" in the Uruguay Round of multilateral negotiations. Because tariffs are not the main focus of these negotiations, discussions have stressed respect for intellectual-property rights and easier movement of specialized professionals as well as capital across international boundaries. None of these concerns involves regulations or other barriers normally administered at the border, except for immigration laws. The economic superpowers realize that their future comparative advantage depends on "inventive and innovative" endowments. These endowments must find expression in a stream of new ideas, and the goods and services which embody them. Many of these ideas will lead to highly specialized innovations, which must make a return for their creators over a short enough period that their economic life is not curtailed by obsolescence. Often, only a world market is worth considering in such a competitive struggle.

In general, firms dealing in technology-intensive goods and services have no interest in conventional tariffs. The kinds of protection they seek are government purchasing policies favoring domestic products, especially in the case of defense goods and some other goods for which public agencies are principal buyers. Such firms are also interested in patent and copyright laws that ensure a period of monopoly rents for their distinctive products and related services. The devil they want to exorcize is counterfeit trade — the practice of putting out exact or nearly exact replicas of a well-known and reliable brand. The illegal replication of high-value products such as computers and top-of-the-line watches is common in some East Asian countries, as is the copying of well-known designer-label clothing items, tape recordings, and computer programs. Trade in generic prescription drugs, while not as illegal as the above practices, also challenges the pharmaceutical producers.

How are these practices to be reduced or controlled? The purist's answer is that property rights should be stronger and effectively enforced. But whose? What scope is there for variety in practice? This is the subject matter of the current GATT debate. Reportedly, the major economic powers have made progress toward consensus among themselves in the intellectual-property negotiations, but there is less evidence that the

NIEs and other countries find their stands to be acceptable. There are numerous issues on which the policies of countries at different stages of development can differ — patent duration and terms, for example. Of particular concern to developing countries are the health-related costs of patent royalties on pharmaceuticals, for which price elasticity of demand is near zero, and monopoly profits are therefore easier to achieve.

It is most unlikely that developing countries, with little near-term prospect of developing intellectual-property rights on their exportables, will have the same interest in protecting monopolies held in more advanced countries — at least, on terms established by those countries. On the other hand, the NIEs are now moving into high-tech activity, and can anticipate future opportunities to benefit from intellectual-property rights. In this respect, they resemble Canada, which has also become increasingly interested in exploiting similar opportunities. Also like Canada, they will continue to be importers of much of the technology they require, and can thus be expected to seek middle ground on issues relating to patents, copyright, and trademarks.[8] There has been considerable disagreement between the United States and individual NIEs and ASEAN countries concerning these matters. Accordingly, if the GATT negotiations are to produce an outcome that will satisfy the developing countries, Canada can play a mediating role based on its experience as an emerging, though selective, producer of high-tech goods and services.

## Trade in Services

On the subject of trade in services, Canada and the NIEs are again on middle ground. Canadians spend as large a share of

---

8 The Canadian debate since the 1960s on pharmaceutical patents and licensing reflects this ambivalence. See Donald G. McFetridge and H.E. English, "Intellectual Property and the GATT Negotiations: Some Areas of Discussion," in English, ed., *Pacific Initiatives in Global Trade*, pp. 159–172.

their disposable income on services as any country (nearly 70 percent). Many services are nontraded, but among those that are traded, Canada is a large net importer. Even when one excludes the servicing of international debt, Canada is in substantial deficit. This deficit mainly reflects a trade in management (including marketing), finance, and technical (applied science and engineering) services — all specialized, skill-intensive activities.

Canada is also a substantial exporter of some traded services — especially science and engineering services related to natural resource development, communications, and the transport sectors. Canadian industrial technology management sees Canadian firms as "niche-fillers" in many of these activities. Canadian business in this sector firmly believes that the Canada-U.S. FTA will put Canadian technology-based entrepreneurs on even terms with their U.S. competitors. They have experience in identifying particular market opportunities for specialized goods and services to which the larger U.S. firms might feel it is not worth diverting managerial services that are used to concentrate on the requirements of larger volume product and service markets. Canada will have an opportunity to test these possibilities now that the FTA affords new market access. Statements from small and medium-sized firms have expressed considerable optimism concerning their prospects.[9]

The NIEs of East and Southeast Asia also hope to expand their services trade. In this region, too, the managerial and commercial-financial services are already emerging and recognized, particularly in Hong Kong and Singapore. Science and engineering goods and services are also appearing in these countries and in Taiwan. However, the trade potential of other services is equally, if not more, important for some Asian countries. This includes construction services, civil aviation,

---

9 These same producers experience the greatest financing problems as a result of their greater need to rely on borrowing in the market when interest rates are high.

and tourism. South Korea has a well-developed construction service sector, which exports construction management and labor teams mainly to other Asian countries, especially in the Middle East and Southeast Asia. South Korea, Hong Kong, Thailand, and Singapore all have highly developed passenger airlines services. At least three of them are rated by travellers as among the world's best. Other tourist facilities, including hotels, are of similar quality.

If trade in services is to be liberalized, these Asian countries will want concessions related to areas in which they are already successfully engaged in return for easing restrictions on the import of services from developed countries of the Pacific region and elsewhere. In principle, they can be expected to welcome agreed guidelines on the liberalization of services, but when it comes to their application, sensitive issues will have to be addressed. For example, they may argue that temporary entry of construction teams for the supply of services is analogous to the arrangement in the Canada-U.S. FTA for the temporary presence of suppliers of business services. It will be politically difficult, however, for North America (or even Japan) to grant this access, given the impact on domestic construction workers. Both immigration laws and attitudes of labor unions will reduce the prospects for this concession. As another example, Asian air carriers wishing to expand their services to North America will run up against opposition from U.S. and Canadian airlines that would see little equivalent benefit in landing rights in cities other than the capital in most Asian countries. Only China, among the Asian Pacific countries, now has the right to land in both Western and Eastern Canadian cities on the same flight. Finally, if Asian shipping companies were to seek rights to carry freight between North American ports, they would encounter even more opposition, especially in the United States, where the *Jones Act* serves as a formidable fortress for an uncompetitive industry — a fortress that could not be breached even in the Canada-U.S. negotiations.

While the expansion of intellectual-property rights and the liberalization of trade in services will encounter problems of asymmetry of interests, the developed countries can achieve progress if they are prepared to make concessions in freeing of traditional manufactures trade. We will return to this later.

## Trade-Related Investment Measures

Trade-related investment measures concern all those sectors to which international investment is attracted, not just high-tech sectors and other services. The basic attitude to foreign investment in the Pacific region is highly favorable. There are many regulations that affect foreign-owned firms, but none is intended to exclude them, and much liberalization has been taking place.

The basic problem is how to avoid economically unsound systems of incentive and disincentive. The competitiveness of the incentive systems introduced by the developing countries — tax holidays, investment credits, and so on — amounts to a transfer of income from the poor to the rich. Furthermore, if all competing governments employ relatively equivalent incentives, no reallocation of resources occurs, except perhaps from even poorer countries that can least afford the transfers. Disincentive systems are less competitive. They are justified only if they reflect the generally held preferences in the nation whose government has introduced them, or at least those of political leaders who have widespread support. Such preferences differ from country to country, and some countries whose governments have not discouraged investment will enjoy economic benefits as a consequence. Developing countries with interventionist inclinations and fairly common development aims may find it advantageous to try to harmonize those incentives and disincentives systems so that policy instruments chosen are efficient in their objectives and do little collateral damage to the development process. A meeting in Bangkok sponsored by PECC in April 1986 discussed this kind of harmonization, and it was in principle supported by representatives of the developed and developing countries present. The Asian countries' commitment to cooperate among themselves offers them an opportunity to demonstrate the feasibility of policy that will reduce the cost to them of at least the more expensive investment incentives practices. In fact, there has been no follow-up to the 1986 meeting, an indication that governments are less willing to resist the temptation to duplicate the incentives of other governments than to pursue collective action to reduce such wasteful transfers.

The role of trade negotiations in investment regulation is much narrower. It is generally agreed that the main object of the current trade talks is to reduce the most direct distortions that may result from national practices — such as those that require foreign-controlled companies to export as a condition of establishment or to guarantee a specified share of host-country content in the value of their production. This does not mean that policies applied to all investing or established firms must be avoided. "National treatment" — that is, treating foreign firms in a manner equivalent to domestic firms — is the standard most likely to be accepted.

## Institutional Improvements in the GATT

This subject encompasses several types of reform. Some are implicit in the foregoing discussion. For example, the virtual exemption of agricultural negotiations during the early years of the GATT is no longer tolerable, and the addition of the new issues discussed above — services, trade-related intellectual property and investment measures — in the Uruguay Round constitutes a potentially major extension of the GATT's scope.

More closely associated with the rules, procedures, and organization of the GATT are several other negotiating groups of the Uruguay Round. Of the 15 negotiating groups presently operating, nearly half are addressing these matters. They include:

- *GATT articles*: proposals to strengthen certain parts of the agreement — for example, trade restrictions for balance-of-payments reasons and the treatment of state trading;
- efforts to improve *GATT codes* established at previous negotiating sessions — for example, those on antidumping, standards, customs valuation, and government procurement;
- better definition of *safeguard actions* — temporary measures to meet import "surges";
- means of *limiting subsidy and countervail measures* to prevent trade distortion through national subsidy practices or to overreact through countervail action;
- *reform of dispute settlement procedures*, to make more certain high and uniform quality in the panels selected for this purpose, and better implementation of their recommendations; and
- the functioning of the GATT system, including better measures for *coordinating and monitoring* trade policy by the better integration of GATT activities with those of other multilateral bodies affecting trade, through monetary policies — that is, through the International Monetary Fund — and investment and aid practices; also, within the GATT, to institute regular trade policy review of national practices and to make those practices better known — that is, to improve their *transparency*.

The Pacific countries have an interest in all of these, but discussions within the region have paid greater attention to a few of them. Safeguard actions are generally considered by East Asian countries as preferable to bilateral arrangements such as voluntary export restraints that are unacceptable under the GATT. Pacific countries are particularly anxious to enhance the temporary aspect of safeguards and to ensure that they are not used to discriminate against the trade of particular countries, a practice that is favored in Europe. Antidumping and countervail practices are also sometimes used against Asian exports instead of safeguards, so that, for Pacific countries, a clearer definition of actionable subsidies is of special interest.

# Translating Pacific Trade Concerns into Action

This brings us to the end of this review of the Pacific region's main concerns in the Uruguay Round. In the light of this discussion, it is possible to identify certain conclusions, or directives for further enquiry.

## Primary Resources Trade

There is scope for widespread agreement on the liberalization of primary resources trade, including that in processed natural products. The main challenges are to eliminate export subsidies resulting from surplus production in highly protected agricultural sectors, to reduce agricultural protectionism supporting the least competitive agricultural products, and to "de-escalate" protection that affects some processed products.

## Traditional Manufactures

Trade in traditional manufactures must be liberalized, particularly in response to the interests of developing countries with comparative advantages in labor-intensive products, including clothing and the less complex metal (and plastic) products. Developed countries may continue to produce the more capital-intensive products in these sectors — primary textiles and basic steel. However, instead of relying on sales to protected clothing industries and those producing "low-tech" metal products, they should encourage sales — mainly through trade liberalization — to more labor-intensive industries in the NIEs and other developing countries. If possible, they should also encourage the further development of Canadian industries that are less labor-intensive users of primary textiles and steel — for example, specialized industrial textiles and high-tech steel products.

In the automobile and consumer durables sectors, which are characterized by component production, product innovation, and marketing, Pacific regional rationalization can provide the following roles:

- developed countries can take the lead in product improvement, design and marketing, high-tech component manufacture, and assembly of those models most in demand in high-income markets;

- developing countries can expect to participate increasingly in the manufacture, at first, of simpler or more labor-intensive components and, in the case of the larger markets, in the assembly of those vehicles most in demand. The success of this program will depend on trade liberalization and encouragement of the environment for investment planning by major firms so that a variety of national economies can play complementary, economically valid roles involving only the necessary minimum of subregional infant-industry support.

## Trade Rules Related to Processing and Manufacturing

For both the developed and the developing countries, trade rules governing subsidies, countervailing duties, and antidumping measures have become priority issues. They are relevant both to resource-based trade and to traditional and more technology-intensive manufactures.[10] In the Pacific, many countries have experienced the discriminatory use of these measures. Japanese exports to Europe, for example, have been singled out for highly protectionist antidumping measures. China has received similar treatment from both Europe and North America.[11]

Although these issues have been the subject of GATT negotiations prior to the Uruguay Round, much remains to be done to ensure that such measures are not applied capriciously or dictated by political priorities rather than by any real abuse of competitive market forces. In the Uruguay Round, an effort is being made to distinguish between "actionable" and "nonactionable" subsidies.[12] Canada's proposals are designed to seek general GATT consensus that could be helpful in the future subsidy-countervail negotiations left incomplete in the Canada-U.S. FTA.[13] Clearly, this is a case where multilateral talks could limit the degree of bilateral dispute over this issue, since Canada's position is closer to that of most other GATT

---

10 See Jean-François Bence and Murray G. Smith, "Subsidies and the Trade Laws: The Canada-U.S. Dimension," *International Economic Issues* (Institute for Research on Public Policy) April-May 1989. This study shows a generally similar pattern in the use of subsidies in both Canada and the United States, though the level is somewhat higher in Canada. Other sources indicate that if the subsidy equivalent of government procurement practices is added, the subsidies to high-technology industries would be even higher. See the April 1990 issue of the same series for an analysis of state and provincial subsidies in North America.

11 On Japan, see Brian Hindley, "Anti-Dumping Action: How the GATT is Threatened," in Smith, ed., *Canada, The Pacific and Global Trade*, pp. 129–144, especially p. 130. On China, see Cai Wenguo, "Canadian and U.S. Anti-dumping Laws and Chinese Exports," *World Competition: Law and Economics Review* 14 (September 1990).

12 Actionable subsidies are best illustrated as those that discriminate in favor of particular firms or sectors. Nonactionable subsidies are those that provide general support for all primary or manufacturing activity.

13 See Smith, ed., *Canada, The Pacific and Global Trade*, Annex I.

partners than to that of the U.S. government, and especially to the position reflected in U.S. congressional proposals.

As noted above, the use and abuse of all trade rules will also be affected by the safeguards negotiations in the Uruguay Round. At the same time, however, the Pacific countries have called for more frequent use of temporary safeguards to control import surges rather than other "escape" measures, provided that there is a clear commitment to the early phasing out of such measures, and an inducement to adjustment in industries affected by import surges.

There is scope for a strong Pacific consensus position in this matter. Furthermore, if the outcome of the Uruguay Round is unsatisfactory, negotiation of Pacific codes might be explored to limit antidumping, countervail, and voluntary export restraints. Such codes, however, would have to be substantially more trade liberalizing than existing GATT practice, and they have to be open to other GATT members that are ready to accept their liberal terms.

## Trade in Services

The Uruguay Round can be expected to reach a general framework agreement identifying the principles that should govern the application of the GATT to trade in services. This might be accompanied by agreement to a "standstill" on existing restrictions on such trade, and an obligation to negotiate compensation on any new restrictions. But sectoral arrangements will be considered necessary to accommodate the diversity of regulations governing services. Only in such sector agreements is there likely to be a basis for holding the line or reducing the most serious of existing trade barriers. Arrangements for some sectors may be more amenable to earlier negotiation — for example, management and consulting services — since public institutions and regulations are not much involved. For others, commitments to discriminatory national policy — for example, in the regulation of shipping and civil aviation — are of long standing. In some cases, Pacific cooperation could lead to policy harmonization agreements.[14] It is expected the exploration of sectoral arrangements will remain a priority after the conclusion of the Uruguay Round.

## Institutional Strengthening of the GATT

Although much of what is discussed above is essential to the strengthening of the GATT, there are certain issues that are directed particularly at the improvement of the institution itself — that is, how to strengthen GATT's authority and expand its influence to less active members and nonmembers. Some issues, such as better dispute-settlement procedures and superior monitoring of national trade policies and practices, serve the interests of all who support an open world trading system — particularly the smaller countries, whose well-being is likely to be most aided by international adjudication and information sources not dominated by the larger economic powers. These are issues on which there is general agreement among Pacific countries.

Of particular importance to the Pacific, however, is the role of China in the GATT. Since the cornerstone of China's new open-door policy is closer integration in the world economy, and especially in that of the Pacific region, the terms governing its expanded trade will be important. How can a centrally planned economy be a "fair trader"? By what criteria are its prices to be accepted as reflecting real economic costs? Decisions made on questions such as these will affect not only China's role in the international system, but also that of other

14 See, for example, Edward P. Neufeld, "Trade in Financial Services and the Uruguay Round," in English, ed., *Pacific Initiatives in Global Trade*, pp. 199–222.

"socialist" economies in the region — the Indo-Chinese countries, North Korea, and, in the future, the Soviet Union. [15]

## Other Priorities in Pacific Economic Cooperation

One of the familiar themes of recent international economics has been the importance of better harmonization of macroeconomic policies. The experience of the mid-1980s is clear evidence of the importance of understanding the sources of macro-maladjustment in the international economy and how it can generate irrelevant protectionism. Lawrence Krause and Sueo Sekiguchi, referring to the origins of the present concerns and actions, have stated:

> The failure of Japan and the United States to respect limits on their macroeconomic policies was the major cause of the economic problems that surfaced between them in the 1970s and caused severe problems for other countries both in and outside the Pacific basin. [16]

The coordination of macroeconomic policies is already promoted through the work of such bodies as the International Monetary Fund, the Organisation for Economic Co-operation and Development, and the Group of Seven. What, then, is the role of regional Pacific cooperation in this economic policy area, where multilateralism seems even more fundamental than it does in trade policy?

The answer again centers on leadership: the activities of the world's two largest economies — the United States and Japan — were fundamental in accentuating the problems of the 1970s and 1980s, but also in making some progress toward

---

15 See J.E.D. McDonnell, "China's Entry into GATT," in English, ed., *Pacific Initiatives in Global Trade*, pp. 247–264.

16 Lawrence B. Krause and Sueo Sekiguchi, eds., *Economic Interaction in the Pacific* (Washington, D.C.: Brookings Institution, 1980).

correcting them. Anything that can be done to regularize the process of macroeconomic accommodation between these two countries will help to avoid inappropriate policy actions in the future. In particular, there should be an effort toward mutual agreement on the implications of new economic shocks — including events such as the food and oil price "leaps" of the early 1970s, or the Persian Gulf conflict — that are not mere repeats of familiar experience.

A regular system of macroeconomic analysis and consultation might help to anticipate problems before they come as "shocks"; it might also define procedures that would be ready to operate, and thus be less *ad hoc* and perhaps less dominated by short-term political considerations. Furthermore, the role of other Pacific countries in discussions about the region's economic outlook and relevant macroeconomic policy harmonization can be useful in leading toward a wider consensus than might otherwise be possible if decisions rested mainly on the views of the United States and Japan. Often, the decisions taken by these two economic superpowers have consequences for smaller countries in the region that may not have been considered. The smaller countries can also add new dimensions — perhaps relating to commodity supply or market conditions — that are central to the interests and health of a majority of Pacific countries.

Another practical consequence of efforts of Pacific countries to develop a coherent regional economic outlook is that it would constitute a pioneer effort to improve and reconcile statistical systems among developed and developing countries. The growing importance of North-South linkages argues for a concerted effort to achieve a strong informational basis for macroeconomic policy coordination. The incompatibility of estimates of investment activity is a notorious example of the inadequacy of present statistical data.

In the past three years, PECC has set up a task force on the Pacifoc economic outlook, with joint U.S.-Japanese leadership. It plans to issue an annual report reflecting a regional perspective involving input from all member committees. The main emphasis will be on reconciling national forecasts, and on using and supplementing existing models that link national estimates. Attention will also be paid to structural issues that play a significant role in the macro outlook. It is expected that some of these will emerge from the PECC Trade Forum and commodity task forces. The first three outlook reports have been issued, the most recent in April 1990, and have received very positive reviews.[17]

An important challenge for the Pacific outlook enterprise will be to include a forecast of China's interaction with its Pacific partners. Attempts to measure this relationship more accurately could play an important part in defining China's role in the world economy. Lessons learned here could also be applied to analyses of actual or potential interactions between the Soviet Union and the Pacific countries. Assessing the implications of the greater convertibility of the Chinese and Soviet currencies could also be an important future activity of the Pacific outlook task force. One can have little doubt that the explanation of macroeconomic linkages between transforming planned economies and "mixed" economies will further encourage the participation of the Soviet Union, as well as that of the Indo-Chinese states and North Korea, in PECC activities.

## Related PECC Initiatives

It was recognized that both trends and macroeconomic relations in the Pacific region are much affected by conditions in commodity sectors. PECC task force activity has particularly addressed those related to supply and other market conditions in agriculture, fisheries, minerals, and energy. While the Trade

---

17 Pacific Economic Cooperation Conference, *Pacific Economic Outlook, 1989–1990* (Washington, D.C.; San Francisco: United States National Committee for Pacific Economic Cooperation, 1989).

Policy Forum has paid particular attention to policies affecting the efficient operation of international markets, specialists in commodity sector conditions have been mainly concerned with domestic supply conditions.

In agriculture, studies and discussions have centered on the restructuring of agricultural activity so as to make more efficient use of arable land. In crowded countries of East Asia, for example, emphasis on those products that can be efficiently developed using land intensively has been recommended, while products such as feed grains and beef are often exported more economically by land-rich countries.

In fisheries, the fuller realization of potential, especially of the South Pacific, has been a focus of attention, particularly with regard to the sharing of technology between the South Pacific islands, ASEAN, and South American countries such as Peru. More recently, this PECC task force has also given some consideration to the question of drift-net fishing in the North Pacific, mostly by Japanese, Taiwanese, and South Korean fleets. Control of this practice now seems more likely.

Petroleum is the only major mineral product of which the Pacific region is a net importer. Accordingly, the Minerals and Energy Forum of PECC was born out of concern about the uncertainty surrounding public policies and corporate investment activity following the near-collapse of oil prices in 1982–83. The Forum has a particular interest in the large companies that play such an important role in the trade of these products. For their part, the large multinational enterprises in this sector have been interested in better access to market information concerning demand, new production potential, and shifts in government policy that can reduce the uncertainties and resulting peaks and troughs of investment and prices. The Forum has also paid special attention to China's development plans for these sectors.

Another PECC activity that has attracted business attention is the so-called Triple-T task force. This is an initiative of the Japanese national committee, and it encompasses transportation, telecommunications, and tourism. In some of these areas, both developed and developing countries have an interest. Singapore, Thailand, South Korea, and Hong Kong are well known as effective competitors in civil aviation, for example, while Malaysia and South Korea, among others, are active in shipping. Most of the region is engaged in the tourist trade, and several of these countries have hotel chains that operate beyond their domestic markets. Governments all around the Pacific are also active in promoting and regulating these sectors, often in ways that distort what the market would dictate, so that this task force could play a useful role in helping to achieve a more rational and harmonized policy pattern — one that is compatible with the more efficient distribution of private investment and resulting services.

Finally, a task force on Science and Technology has been established, co-chaired by the Chinese and U.S. national committees, which is examining "policy and industry practice in the areas of the transfer of technology, the funding of basic research and [industrial] R&D, technology trade, [and] intellectual property rights." The objectives include exchange of information and analyses of investment plans and market conditions in the technology-intensive sectors, the "training and exchange of scientists", and "industrial research collaboration and coordination of R&D and investments."

In the past, international technology transfer has been handled on a bilateral basis, with intense competition among the businesses and governments of the larger economic powers. There is some danger, however, that such competition can lead to an expensive, wasteful rivalry for which smaller importers of technology could be asked to pay. Some of these countries might be induced to evade such costs through technology "piracy", a practice that has already generated bilateral disputes in the region and in the GATT negotiations on trade-related intellectual property issues. Some convergence of policies to accommodate both appropriate reward for innovation and the development priorities of the smaller technology importers is likely to continue to be important beyond the Uruguay Round. The Science and Technology task force, with the participation of science policy planners, can play a leadership role in this regard.

# 3

# Canada's Stake
# in Pacific Cooperation

Canada is often a little late in taking advantage of its opportunities. While others prepare for the Pacific century, Canada is still preoccupied with its North American relations, and even with its traditional European connections. These preoccupations are perfectly understandable, but nevertheless regrettable. We must learn to "walk and chew gum" at the same time or, to put it less colorfully, "to act in the present and plan for the future."

Fortunately, Canada is so well endowed with natural and human resources that there are still opportunities waiting to be seized. Canadians were recently reminded of this by the report of an Investment Study Mission organized by Keidanren, Japan's most prestigious business organization.[1] The charac-

---

[1] See Japanese Investment Study Mission to Canada, *Canada, A Nation Challenging the World* (Tokyo, 1989). This widely circulated, 25-page report, backed by a much larger document, was prepared under the chairmanship of Shinroku Morohashi, President of Mitsubishi Corporation and Acting Chairman of the Japan-Canada Economic Committee of Keidanren. However, in the *Globe and Mail*, May 16, 1990, a report on the most recent annual meeting of Canadian and Japanese businessmen reflects the new concern...

teristic Canadian reaction, from both business and government, was that the title — *Canada, A Nation Challenging the World* — was too pretentious. So far as being prepared to grasp Pacific opportunities and adapt to Pacific challenges are concerned, Canada is clearly well back in the competition.

This chapter focuses on Canada's stake in the Pacific region. In particular, it addresses the following issues:

- What are Canada's objectives in the region?
- What is the present state of Canada's trading relationships with the countries of the region and with the regional organizations now in existence?
- What are the main priorities that Canada should address in the next few years in order to strengthen our chances of achieving its trade objectives?
- What are the main capital flows between Canada and other Pacific countries and the prospects for the future of investment in the region?

## Canada's Objectives in the Pacific Region

To identify these objectives, one should examine both stated government policies and the actions of government, which often speak louder than words.

Only occasionally has the federal government provided a comprehensive statement of its international economic objectives. In the early years of the Trudeau government, it pub-

---

1 - *cont'd.*

...that recent agreement on measures to reduce some U.S.-Japan frictions will leave Canada on the sidelines because of the lack of sufficient Canadian initiatives and because of new deterrents to investments in Canada, including the constitutional crisis.

lished booklets on foreign policy that, in effect, reaffirmed Canada's self-perception as a middle power devoted to serving its own security and prosperity, and to making a contribution to global efforts primarily through multilateral institutions. In the 1970s, the link between Canada's continental interdependence and its global interests was exploited by private and public groups. Trudeau's abortive "third option" in the early 1970s sought to move away from North American economic integration by developing some kind of special relationship with Europe. This notion, however, was doomed to fail: How could the Europeans grant special status to Canada without doing the same for the United States? Throughout this time, the government paid lip service to the importance of improving economic ties with the Pacific region, but a strongly Eurocentric Department of External Affairs virtually ignored the potential in that direction.

The merger of the Department of External Affairs and the Department of Industry, Trade and Commerce led to an increased focus on the economics side of Canada's foreign relations and, in particular, on the growing importance of the Pacific — a region in which its political interests had waned since the end of the Korean War.

In recent years, Canada has pursued a three-track policy that places equal emphasis — at least politically — on relations with the United States, Europe, and the Asia-Pacific region, the "three principal pillars" of Canada's economic relations. Prime Minister Mulroney, in a speech in Singapore in October 1989, explained the government's new "Going Global" program:

> "Going Global" is a program of some $94 million worth of new trade and investment and science and technology initiatives, designed to position Canada strategically in the major markets — the United States, Asia-Pacific and Europe.
> The Asia-Pacific dimension of the new policy — called "Pacific 2000" — and budgeted for up to $65 million in new funds over five years — will promote Canada-Pacific business links, upgrade Canadian skills in Asian cultures and lan-

guages, provide for increased cooperation in science and technology and encourage exchange programs.[2]

In an earlier address, in May 1989, Secretary of State for External Affairs Joe Clark outlined in more detail the Pacific 2000 program:

- a trade strategy designed to maintain and improve our own market share;
- a Japan Science and Technology Fund;
- an Asian Languages and Awareness Fund; and
- a Pacific 2000 Projects Fund which will offer support to Canadian activities in the region.

Noting that Canada is "a player whose trans-Pacific economic, political, security and cultural links are dramatically expanding," Mr. Clark then elaborated on the program's aims:

- mustering support for liberalized global trade;
- promoting common disciplines and rules on trade, investment, technology transfer and intellectual property;
- research and analysis of regional economic growth;
- engaging in scientific cooperation in areas of common interest; and
- ensuring that the Pacific Rim countries are integrated into the international economy.[3]

This statement implies that the federal government sees the Pacific as playing a leadership role to preserve the multilateral trading system and to develop new rules to govern those aspects of economic relations that are not yet guided by an institutional regime.

Events since the summer of 1989 will add further agenda items to the program. These include the implications for other Pacific partners of the proposed U.S.-Mexico free trade negoti-

---

2 Rt. Hon. Brian Mulroney, Address to the Institute for Southeast Asian Studies, Singapore, October 15, 1989.

3 Rt. Hon. Joe Clark, "Canadian Partnership in Pacific 2000," Ottawa, May 16, 1989.

ations, including Canada's particular role in those negotiations; and the implications of events in Europe for the region, especially the diversion of investment and official aid from projects in the developing economies. Finally, there is the reordering of U.S. priorities in response to events in the Middle East and the implications of the oil price increase and related uncertainties. All of these events could contribute to a greater emphasis on Western Pacific solidarity and to some decline in U.S. participation in Pacific institution building. On the other hand, the importance of Japanese economic support for Eastern European and Middle East initiatives argues for the continued strengthening of the U.S.-Japan partnership. The event that can affect this the most — for good or ill — is the success or failure of the Uruguay Round. If it falls seriously short of the goals the United States has set for it, the bilateral policies that the U.S. Congress has threatened to apply more vigorously (super-301, for example) will certainly endanger trans-Pacific economic relations, and not only *vis-à-vis* Japan.

None of this changes the importance of Pacific regional cooperation for Canada. Its challenge is to help ensure a continued active and constructive role in linking Pacific interests to relevant global priorities.

## The Political Dimension

At the political level, Canada generally seeks to balance independence and managed interdependence. In this new era of multipolarity, its economic and political security depends on a complex pattern of political associations involving its special bilateral relationship with the United States, multilateral institutions, regional cooperation, and specific-issue alliances.

In the Pacific, Canada's political role appears to center on forging or reinforcing links among new and old partners. This country should develop a "middle man" role between the main Pacific partners, as it did between the major Atlantic powers during World War II and in the early postwar years. The fact that Canada has not yet established its credentials for this endeavor does not mean that it is too late to try. Canada cannot afford to be idle, since any breakdown in Japanese-U.S. cooperation would be costly for this country as well. But Canada can also be active in encouraging Japan's reconciliation with the Soviet Union and South Korea's relations with China and the Soviet Union. The ability of the Soviet Union to move toward a mixed economy capable of participating in Pacific trade and development cooperation will be enhanced by settlement of the "northern territories" issue with Japan. This will open up access to Japanese technology, including an industrial and bureaucratic management system probably better suited to the transactions of a centrally directed economy.

Canada should also be active in promoting the involvement of Mexico and other new members of the Pacific Economic Cooperation Conference (PECC). The more effective participation of Eastern Pacific countries in institution building in the region will be better assured if this task does not fall on the United States alone.

More generally, Canada should support the gradual evolution of greater democracy in all the major newly industrializing economies (NIEs) and developing countries of East Asia. There will be opportunities for specific initiatives that help that evolutionary trend, while encouraging the patience and gradualism that accommodate political and cultural realities and reinforce the efforts of practical reformers in East Asian societies. Canada enjoys goodwill in the area that no other middle-sized nation of the region can quite match. But goodwill must be complemented by relevant knowledge and determination.

## The Economic Dimension

Canada's scope for a measure of political independence in international affairs depends not only on its skill in diplomacy, but also on its economic strength. This in turn depends on the efficiency with which the Canadian economy is managed. Canada has elected to base its prosperity on managed inter-dependence — through multilateral instruments such as the International Monetary Fund, the General Agreement on Tariffs and Trade, and the Organisation for Economic Co-operation and Development; and through regional instruments, the most notable of which is the Canada-U.S. Free Trade Agreement (FTA). This agreement, in fact, goes beyond any liberalization of trade possible in the multilateral system. In this respect, it follows the example of the European Community (EC). Unlike the EC, however, Canada is more interested in using efficiency gains achieved through access to the larger U.S. market (and the challenge of increased competition) to build its competitive strength in overseas markets, particularly in East Asia. Canadians thus should be motivated not only to support the shift of capital into industries that can compete in both the United States and the Pacific, but also to encourage the opening up of its own market exporters from East and Southeast Asia. This will benefit Canadian consumers and establish firm ground on which to build Canada's participation in Pacific initiatives that will reduce its dependence on purely North American economic relationships.

The economic aspect of Canada's political effort to forge links between the market economies of East Asia and the centrally planned economies of China and the Soviet Union might be manifested in joint ventures involving Canadian firms with partners from Japan or South Korea in resource development projects (in Siberia, for example). This is a region where Canada's prospects for playing an effective role are much greater than in Eastern Europe, where Germany and other EC countries have a substantial advantage.

The economic aspects of Canada's promotion of a more active role for Latin American countries in the Pacific relates to the mutual interest these countries and Canada have in

resource development and the possibility of convergent interests in trade arrangements for the control of nontariff barriers,
macroeconomic policy coordination, and the harmonization of
policies affecting investment and trade in services.

In summary, Canada now has a tremendous opportunity
to develop its political and economic links with the Pacific
region. These links would act as a counterweight to Canada's
bilateral relationship with the United States and as a catalyst
in strengthening multilateral institutions.

## Canada's Current Economic
## Relations with the Pacific Region

Canada is well regarded in the Pacific, and has amicable
relations with all countries in the region. As a member of the
Commonwealth, it shares certain institutions and attitudes
with four of PECC's largest members — Australia, New Zealand,
Malaysia, and Singapore — and with some of the Pacific island
states. Canada also has a long record of providing economic
and development assistance to various countries in the region
— including Indonesia, South Korea, Thailand, China, and the
countries of Indo-China. This assistance has come from official
sources as well as from nongovernmental organizations. An
indication of the importance Canada has attached to its relations with the region is the fact that its embassy in Tokyo was
just the second it opened after becoming fully responsible for
its own external affairs.

For Canada, as for the United States, the value of trans-
Pacific trade surpassed trans-Atlantic trade in the 1980s (see
Table 2 for a breakdown of Canada's trade by region). Private
investment has also grown steadily, especially Japanese investment in Canada, but also Canadian investment in Southeast Asia and Australia.

Table 2 shows vividly that 85 percent of Canada's exports
are destined for its partners in the PECC. Even when the United

## Table 2

### *The Origin and Destination of Canada's Trade, 1988*

(C$ millions)

|  | Exports (and % of total) | Imports | Balance |
|---|---|---|---|
| United States | $101,008 (73.1) | $86,509 | $6,486 |
| Main Western Pacific Economies (members of PECC) | 16,773 (12.1) | 18,291 | –1,518 |
| Western Europe | 12,801 (9.3) | 18,890 | –6,029 |
| Latin America and the Caribbean | 3,112 (2.3) | 4,541 | –1,424 |
| Eastern Europe | 1,401 (1.0) | 614 | 787 |
| Africa, Middle East, and South Asia | 2,899 (2.1) | 1,736 | 1,162 |
| *Total trade* | *138,150 (100.0)* | *131,604* | *6,486* |

Note:  Negative figures indicate an excess of imports over exports. Percentages do not add up to 100 due to rounding.

Source:  Canada, Department of External Affairs.

States is excluded, the figure is still significant. On the import side, while trans-Pacific and trans-Atlantic trade are almost equal, Canada has important nontariff barriers — for example, policies affecting textile products and dairy products imports — that discriminate against Western Pacific countries.

Table A-2 in the Appendix details changes in Canada's export and import totals for Pacific economies. This reveals the shifting patterns, casting some light especially on the probable explanation of the sources and stability of the balances. For example, the period of overvaluation of the U.S. dollar generated huge trade surpluses for Canada. That these did not decline more in the 1986–87 period can be attributed to the restoration of commodity markets, which also dramatically improved trade by the Association of Southeast Asian Nations (ASEAN). This affected both the value of Canada's imports and the volume of exports from the ASEAN region. The revaluation of the yen shows up as a factor in increasing the value of Canadian exports and the decline in imports from Japan.

What are the characteristics of Canada's trade with the Western Pacific? On the export side, trade is still dominated by natural resources in raw and processed forms, reflecting Canada's diverse natural endowments. Among the top six categories of exports to Japan, for example, all four major resource sectors — mining, agriculture, forestry, and fisheries — are represented. The same emphasis on natural products is true for Canada's trade with the NIEs. More highly manufactured products go to China, Hong Kong, and Southeast Asia. South Korea and the ASEAN countries take, in particular, Canadian synthetic rubber, plastic materials, and telecommunications equipment. Some other manufactures — airplane engines, forestry and mining equipment, office machines — are partly or wholly financed by Canada's aid programs in ASEAN countries. The same manufactured products play an important part in commercial exports to Australia and New Zealand. Canadian service sectors are active in the Western Pacific, especially banks, air services, other resource-related scientific and engineering development services, and telecommunications services.

On the import side, Canadian trade with the region is primarily in three groups of products:

- labor-intensive manufactures, especially textile products, shoes, household hardware, and toys mainly from the NIEs, China, and the ASEAN countries;
- consumer durables such as automobiles, consumer electronics, and photographic goods, mainly from Japan and South Korea for the more complex items and from Taiwan, Hong Kong, Singapore, and Malaysia for "basic" items such as radios and television sets;
- tropical natural products, mainly from the ASEAN countries, though sugar and semitropical fruit is also imported from Australia.

Livestock products figure prominently in imports from both Australia and New Zealand. Among the major services supplied from the Western Pacific area are airline and tourist services. Financial services, especially from Japan and Hong Kong, are growing in step with investment from the region.

## The Keys to Canada's Future Pacific Trade Strategy

Except in relation to Australia, New Zealand, and, of course, the United States, Canada's Pacific trade is likely to continue to be driven by its strong comparative advantage in a wide range of natural products and by the strength of the demand for such products by the region's rapidly growing economies. It should be stressed that trade *volume* is demand driven. That is the fundamental reason, along with easy access, for the overwhelming role of the United States in Canada's trade. More assured access to the U.S. market and improved access to the larger Asian markets can have two major effects on Canada's trade.

The major opportunities for new resource-based exports lie in the upgrading and further processing of natural products, and in expanding their accompanying services. This is the most advantageous course for Canada, and is based on the country's two most plentiful endowments: natural resources, and the skills and technology required in their production and use. The extension of exports of technology-intensive products and services related to the resource sector depends on reasonably assured access to one or more larger markets. The reason for this is that products or services of the kind that specialized new technology generates do not often find natural markets comparable to the volume of demand for widely consumed raw materials. They are also subject to technical obsolescence. Therefore, the "winners" will usually be those who can seize a substantial share of the limited international market for their distinctive products or services, and then hang on to or replenish their technological leads for as many products as possible. Access to the U.S. market under the FTA by these kinds of firms is an essential means of obtaining the essential, but still limited — by comparison with larger-volume products — economies of scale they require to be internationally competitive. To capture a small share of a large market may be easier than to acquire a large share of a small market, and therefore a surer way of spreading research and other fixed costs over a large enough volume to be competitive before obsolescence begins to set in. Canada's software companies are a case in point.

For Canada, the role of Pacific markets is to widen opportunities for such products and services. In sectors relating to natural resource production, Canada has a greater comparative advantage relative to Japan than it has relative to the United States, which is more competitive in this sector. In other areas, because Canadian producers are accustomed to dealing with the needs of a smaller market than that which is of prime interest to U.S. firms, Canadian firms sometimes capture markets for specialized products in the United States and elsewhere in the Pacific.

Canada may have some advantages over Japan in meeting market demand in China and Southeast Asia: its greater focus on the specialized development needs of some natural-resource-based activities, and a political advantage over both the United States and Japan as a country without an imperial past. A problem in South Korea and Taiwan has been the "bargaining" strength of the U.S. government as their major source of security. At times, governments in these countries have felt pressured to discriminate in favor of U.S. exports, although it seems likely that this factor will decline in importance in the future.

It must be acknowledged that Canada will continue to be handicapped in the export of manufactures and services not related to natural resources. The point is obvious for labor-intensive goods. Consumer durables are also a problem, although it would be premature to write off this whole sector. Clearly, in the newer and most technology-intensive products — particularly those related to computers — Canada still has an opportunity to compete successfully. The rising value of the Japanese yen against the Canadian dollar (and that of the United States) , in particular, helps to make Canadian (and U.S.) exports of such products more attractive.

Canada's trade with the Pacific is handicapped most fundamentally, however, by the fact that manufactured exports must continue to compete with resource-based exports, which raises the value of the dollar and, therefore, the international price of other manufactures. Resource-poor Japan and South Korea would have an economic advantage even if they were less technically efficient, because the values of their currencies are depressed by their dependency on imports of resource-based products. For the same reason, the ASEAN countries will have a similar difficulty in exporting to Northeast Asia manufactures that are neither resource based nor labor intensive.

## Canada's Role in Pacific Investment

In this section, we examine the recent flows of both direct and portfolio investment in the Pacific region, and the changing role that Canada can play in Pacific investment in the 1990s.

Direct investment basically applies to investment that carries with it a significant measure of management control over enterprises that are established as new, wholly owned or controlled subsidiaries or those that are acquired by takeover or merger. The essential feature of this activity is that it is a major mechanism for the transfer of technology between countries, including basic industrial technology, and management, marketing, and financial skills. The transfer of money capital as such does not require direct investment, but moves in response to differences in national rates of return, taking account of differences in risk and uncertainty, both economic and political. Fundamentally, money is the means by which earnings are derived from the transfer of all kinds of technology. Pools of savings are more characteristic of rich countries, as is upgraded human capital — including that of technical innovations of many kinds. There should be no confusion about the differences in motivation between these types of investment, but there often is, as we shall see later.

The dominance of the rich countries in direct investment is clear from Table 3, which shows direct inflows and outflows into the Pacific economies that are members of PECC. The rich countries' use of savings, however, can be explained only in terms of the technological and skills advantages that they are able to exploit in other countries. Furthermore, they can choose between investment and other forms of technology transfer, by licensing of intellectual property — patents, trademarks, and so on — or by training programs sponsored through official aid, or even by the sale of capital goods. the fact that huge flows of direct investment take place becomes crucial to the realization of technological development.

The table shows the large balance of direct investment inflows in the Pacific region's developing countries. The balance of outflows reflects the coming of maturity to some economies — Canada, Australia, and the United States. But more specific and unique circumstances are reflected in the figures for Japan and the United States.

Japan's massive outflow balance is the result of its very high savings rate and substantial technological advantages. But it is also affected by the motivation to foreign investment in the United States from a combination of higher interest rates, a depreciated U.S. dollar, and fear of increased U.S. protectionism during the years cited in the table. It is true that access to the Japanese market by foreign direct investors from other countries is not made easier by bureaucratic practices and the resistance of Japanese business to joint ventures in Japan. But given the competitive strength of Japanese firms, it is difficult to make a case that the difference between outflows

## Table 3

### Direct Investment from and into Members of the Pacific Economic Co-operation Conference, 1985–88

(millions of Special Drawing Rights; in October 1990, 1 SDR = US$1.44)

|  |  | 1985 | 1986 | 1987 | 1988 |
|---|---|---|---|---|---|
| Australia | *Outflow* | 1,696 | 2,552 | 3,776 | 4,355 |
|  | *Inflow* | 2,018 | 2,593 | 2,086 | 4,012 |
| Canada | *Outflow* | 3,691 | 2,580 | 3,785 | 5,350 |
|  | *Inflow* | −1,712 | 1,143 | 3,307 | 2,889 |
| China | *Outflow* | 619 | 384 | 499 | n/a |
|  | *Inflow* | 1,634 | 1,598 | 1,790 | n/a |
| Indonesia | *Outflow* |  |  |  |  |
|  | *Inflow* | 304 | 221 | 337 | 404 |
| Japan | *Outflow* | 6,332 | 12,223 | 14,995 | 25,485 |
|  | *Inflow* | 616 | 201 | 919 | −355 |
| South Korea | *Outflow* | 33 | 93 | 143 | 113 |
|  | *Inflow* | 227 | 365 | 462 | 649 |
| Malaysia | *Outflow* |  |  |  |  |
|  | *Inflow* | 684 | 417 | 327 | 483 |
| New Zealand | *Outflow* | 60 | 57 | 61 | 68 |
|  | *Inflow* | 152 | 143 | 142 | 157 |
| Philippines | *Outflow* |  |  |  |  |
|  | *Inflow* | 15 | 108 | 237 | 696 |
| Singapore | *Outflow* | 234 | 147 | 174 | 175 |
|  | *Inflow* | 1,031 | 555 | 975 | 968 |
| Chinese Taipei | *Outflow* | 40 | 54 | 91 | 193 |
|  | *Inflow* | 588 | 565 | 1,162 | 825 |
| Thailand | *Outflow* | 1 | 1 | 127 | 18 |
|  | *Inflow* | 159 | 225 | 271 | 832 |
| United States | *Outflow* | 17,462 | 24,084 | 34,027 | 13,070 |
|  | *Inflow* | 18,878 | 28,709 | 36,170 | 43,497 |

Note: A negative figure indicates net divestment.

Sources: International Monetary Fund, *Balance of Payments Statistics Yearbook 1989, Part II* (Washington, D.C.: IMF, 1989); Chinese Taipei (Taiwan) statistics are based on investment approved by the Investment Commission, Ministry of Economic Affairs, Chinese Taipei.

and inflows would be much smaller or that it reflects an economic distortion.

The United States' position in 1988 shows a remarkable departure from previous balances. The decline in the outflow of U.S. investment is partly explained by domestic market conditions favoring the use of its limited savings at home. It should be noted that the U.S. flow figures mask the fact that the huge accumulated U.S. direct investment stock in other countries supports external investment activity, on the basis of reinvested earnings and borrowings in host markets, but this could not markedly modify the sharp change in direction in the 1988 figures.

Canada's role in the aggregate is substantial, though significantly less per capita than, for example, Australia's. Canada has been a net exporter of foreign direct investment in most recent years, notably in 1988. In that year, inflow declined somewhat, as opportunities in Canada may have appeared somewhat less attractive as the Canadian dollar strengthened relative to that of the United States.

The stock of foreign direct investment in Canada is now well over C$110 billion, about 70 percent of which is held by U.S. investors. Britain is the second-largest foreign direct investor in Canada, with about 10 percent of the total stock. The rest of Europe holds an equal share, with Germany and the Netherlands being the leaders — at about 3 percent each — followed by France and Switzerland. Until recent years, Japan's share was only about the same as Germany's. It is now approaching 4.5 percent of the total, which is still well below Britain's share. The total from Pacific-area sources (excluding the United States) is estimated at about US$6 billion; Hong Kong and Australian investors contribute about US$1.7 billion of this total.[4]

---

4 Japan's external direct investment assets reached US$217 billion by 1989. Of this, $85 billion (39 percent of the total) is held in the United States. East Asian investments are almost half as large as those in the United States,...

Direct foreign investment by Canadians now totals about C$45 billion, two-thirds of which is concentrated in U.S. holdings. Among direct investors in the United States, Canada ranks fourth, with 7.6 percent of the total stock. Ahead of it are Britain (with 31.5 percent), Japan (about 17 percent), and the Netherlands (14 percent). Just behind Canada is Germany, with 6.9 percent of the total. In recent years, the shares of Canada and the European countries (except Britain) have declined, while Japan's has risen.

Canada's direct investment in Asia in 1986 was about US$2 billion, or 3.6 percent of the total stock of foreign direct investment in the region. The largest recipient of this Canadian investment was Indonesia (US$1.1 billion); Japan received only US$227 million. Most Canadian investment in the Pacific has been related to the resource sectors. For example, the Indonesian figure is almost entirely the result of International Nickel's mining development in Sulawesi.

Asian direct investment in Canada has also been concentrated in the resource sectors. Much of the earlier Japanese financing of B.C. copper and coal projects was in the form of debt capital. More recently, however, Japanese equity investment — apart from the high-profile auto sector — has been concentrated in pulp and paper; service sectors such as recreational facilities, hotels, and financial institutions; and real estate. Other Asian equity investment in Canada has reflected a similar pattern of priorities — examples include South Korea's Hyundai in automobiles, Chinese investment in a small B.C. pulp mill, and substantial Hong Kong and Taiwanese investment in real estate and recreational facilities.

---

4 - *cont'd.*

...with the leading destinations being Australia ($10.4 billion), Indonesia ($9.8 billion), Hong Kong ($6.2 billion), Singapore ($3.8 billion), South Korea ($3.2 billion), and China ($2.0 billion). Canada's share approached $4 billion in 1989.

Most recently, the federal government's business immigration program has resulted in people from East Asia — notably Hong Kong — setting up numerous smaller enterprises in Canada. It has also meant the possibility of increased trans-Pacific links in trade and investment based on increased familiarity with Asian opportunities and the techniques of entrepreneurship appropriate to Asian markets.

The prospects for this kind of favorable feedback of Canadian-based economic activity in Asia will depend on the continued health of Hong Kong as a private-enterprise economy. In turn, this will depend on the evolution of China's economic policies and on the degree to which it permits a separate economic regime to continue in Hong Kong after that British colony reverts to China in 1997. Favorable signs are Japan's recent announcement that it intends to make investment in China a high priority once more, and the importance it attaches to Hong Kong as a base for its business ventures in South China. China should find it to be to its advantage to accommodate Japanese business interests, and this should greatly enhance the prospects for the continuation of indigenous Chinese private enterprise and for investors and traders from other countries, including Canada.

Canada's role in that region will be enhanced by the Hongkong Bank's base in British Columbia, as well as by other Hong Kong financial interests there, and by the efforts of the new International Finance Centre in Vancouver. These interests are well linked to Chinese business communities not only in China, Hong Kong, and Taiwan, but also in Singapore, Bangkok, Manila, Kuala Lumpur, and Jakarta.

The future of East Asian investment in Canada, viewed from the perspective of the beginning of 1991, is dampened by many uncertainties. One of these is the outcome of the Uruguay Round. Should it fall substantially short of expectations, the forces of protectionism in the United States will almost certainly exert great pressure on Japan and the other strong exporters of East Asia to make their markets more accessible. The U.S. balance-of-payments position will not improve rapidly, especially in the context of new overseas financial commitments in the Middle East, and U.S. attention to the structural problems of its economy may receive lower priority than they should. While the Canada-U.S. FTA is designed to prevent the spillover effects of increased U.S. protectionism, such circumstances will not enhance the prospects for Japanese investment in Canada.

Meanwhile, Canada's own problems with fiscal deficits, lack of federal-provincial economic cooperation, constitutional uncertainty concerning Quebec, the weakness of monetary instruments in dealing effectively with stagnation, and an overvalued dollar all make the short-term outlook less than rosy. It is the ultimate irony that this is happening at a time when Canadian manufacturing industry is gearing to rationalize its operations to achieve greater competitiveness in response to the "carrot-and-stick" effects of the FTA.

The longer-term outlook is more important if one wishes to contemplate Canada's trade and investment prospects in the Pacific region more optimistically. These prospects depend heavily on a healthy base for Canadian industrial and business technology. It is important for all sectors — resources, manufacturing, and services — though clearly much more so for specific subsectors or firms that are technology intensive in these activities. Among Canadian enterprises active in Pacific trade are a number producing specialized products for the resource sectors, and others supplying inputs and services to these sectors — such as distant sensing equipment and services, oceanographic equipment, and engineering services related to the mineral and forest sectors.

Essentially, Canada's comparative advantages rest on two endowments: natural resources, and a technological competence that a middle-sized country can apply selectively to a particular range of goods and services.

As many commentators have stressed, the most important aspect of foreign direct investment inflow is the transfer of technology that accompanies it. This transfer takes many forms. Japanese management practice is one that receives much publicity, but the sharing of industrial technology has the highest profile.

The relatively low level of Canadian industrial research and development (R&D) expenditure as well as the particularly small share — compared with other countries — that is funded by industry are concerns frequently expressed by those who wish to see Canada competing effectively in world markets. In a recent study for the Canada-Japan Trade Council, Charles McMillan notes that there is a need for more consortia involving Canadian scientists from both the private and public sectors, as well as more cooperative research with Japan, "partly because Japanese scientists may feel less threatened with Canadian colleagues than American or European; but mostly because Canada has so much to gain." To achieve this, McMillan says, greater "public support for international education and science" is badly needed. He cites the efforts of U.S. and Australian universities to develop "joint programs in specialized areas such as computers and electronics, and even establishment of foreign campuses," and also notes corporate sponsorship of students through cooperative job and study programs.[5]

Another Canadian academic view, by Professor John Brownlee of the University of Toronto, laments the consequences of provincial control of education and the low priority of the nation's international interests in the allocation of funds.[6]

---

5 Charles J. McMillan, *Investing in Tomorrow: Japan's Science and Technology Organization and Strategies* (Ottawa: Canada-Japan Trade Council, 1989).

6 John Brownlee, in "Canada and Japan: Bilateral Relations in a Global Context" (Proceedings of a conference sponsored by the Canada-Japan Trade Council, Ottawa, November 8, 1989).

One recent federal government study, by the Science Council of Canada, concluded that:

> Canada and Japan [should] immediately pursue a program of enhanced cooperation in the following six broad "umbrella" areas of science and technology. These areas of equal importance are:
>
> • advanced materials and biomaterials;
> • biotechnology and biosciences;
> • oceanography and ocean engineering;
> • space science, technology, and cosmology;
> • advanced manufacturing (artificial intelligence and robotics), microelectronics, communications, and photonics; and
> • sustainable development and environmental management.[7]

The report goes on to specify such means of cooperation as the exchange of information; binational postdoctoral programs and the exchange of graduate students, junior and senior scientists and engineers; binational workshops; access to major science and technology facilities in the two countries; and cooperative R&D projects.

Some of these areas — for example, the first three and the last — relate closely to Canada's special skills in resource sectors, while in others, such as advanced manufacturing, Japan's superiority is clear. The recognition that more Canadian resources will be required to achieve the objective of high-tech cooperation comes at an awkward time for a federal government with a huge fiscal deficit. However, about one-third of the Pacific 2000 program's funds have been assigned to this purpose.

To achieve Canada's potential in these directions fully will require effective partnerships that ensure access to technology that can be traded for what Canadians produce selectively at

---

7 Canada-Japan Committee, *Canada-Japan Complementarity Study* (Ottawa: Science Council of Canada, 1989).

home. That is the underlying theme of the Science Council's report. It is also implicit in the 1989 Keidanren report cited earlier. For Canada to be "a nation challenging the world" — in the rather ambitious words of the report's title — it would have to continue to diversify its resource-products sector, adding higher-value-added products. For Canadians to maximize their achievements in the high-tech sector, they will have to recognize that:

> A healthy technology industry requires not only R&D, but the support of a mature industrial base able to supply the required *components and materials and considerable marketing capabilities*. It is in these areas that Japanese and Canadian industry can complement each other and that the profitable and comprehensive development of our economies may be possible.[8]

Interpreting this and reading between the lines, Canada's priorities are to strengthen its domestic technological endowments while establishing and expanding channels of access to Asian — especially Japanese — technology through investment and technological cooperative arrangements. In this way, it would be possible to increase Canadian exports of technology-intensive goods and services, as well as joint ventures or other investments that exploit complementary production and marketing capabilities.

A case in point is Lumonics, a profitable and growing Canadian firm in the vanguard of applied laser technology, which found itself unable to resist a takeover by the Japanese firm Sumitomo. Among the basic reasons for this were the immense costs — for a firm with $100 million in business — in maintaining its technological lead and in defending itself against a patent infringement suit originating in the United States. A challenge to Canadian interest in this case is whether

---

8 Japanese Investment Study Mission to Canada, *Canada, A Nation Challenging the World.*

Canada's specific technological endowments can be maintained, or whether the parent firm will, in effect, move all further R&D to its head office facilities.

## Conclusion

This chapter has addressed trade and investment issues affecting Canada's Pacific interests and opportunities. It is perhaps most important to emphasize that the relationship between trade and investment is complex, and that Canadian expectations should be assessed in a realistic context. Foreign direct investment is not uniformly spread among all industrial sectors; it is concentrated mainly in sectors where one or more of the following three conditions give distinct advantages to the larger, regionally dispersed or product-diversified firm:

- where risk is high and needs to be spread over a range of activities;
- where technological change is rapid, R&D costs are high relative to production and other costs, and intellectual-property rights can be acquired in several markets; and
- where marketing constitutes a significant share of the firm's total outlays and intellectual property rights can be acquired in dispersed markets.

The first of these conditions applies to certain resource industries — especially in the energy and minerals sectors, and to some extent the forest products sector — where the costs of exploration and development may be high, and where the risks of failure arise out of uncertainty about the quality or quantity of the resource discovered and the volatility of prices. Among Canada's natural resource industries, foreign direct investment spreads such risks among dispersed operations. Since it leads directly to export potential, investment is fully complementary to trade in these sectors. The future of investment in

Canada is related to the growth of demand and the availability of new resources at competitive prices. In these sectors, both Canadian and foreign-based multinationals are active, and important opportunities remain for external expansion, especially in areas where foreign enterprise has not had ready access in the past — for example, in China and Siberia. For the near future, however, political uncertainties and a lack of infrastructure, particularly in Siberia, will remain a handicap.

In the technology-intensive sectors, the kind of linkage described above between Canadian and Japanese — as well as U.S. — firms will be essential to both trade and investment activity. It should be added that where this consideration is dominant, outward foreign investment is relatively rare for the smaller partner. Trade for Canadian-based firms is the more likely option and then only for selected products. Investment is more likely initiated by the larger partner and may then be mainly designed to acquire technology that can then be incorporated into its technological arsenal. Continuing benefits to the smaller partner will be greater if it retains specialized R&D capacity and/or a "world product mandate" or its equivalent.

In marketing-intensive industries, dispersal of activity is more likely. For consumer products and services, the importance of trademarks has meant that a relatively few brand-name products based in the largest economies will retain their dominant positions. Inflow of foreign investment is likely in such sectors, since product modification and marketing strategy are often adapted to differences in consumer tastes. The market size for many consumer products is sufficiently large so that economies of scale can be achieved in markets served by branchplants. This dispersion of production was also orginally encouraged by the higher protection applied to consumer goods. Reduction or removal of protection typically requires a reduction of diversification in such plants, but also typically the expansion of those product lines best suited to market or supply conditions in the host country. This kind of adaptation has been evident in the early response to the Canada-U.S. FTA.

For more specialized goods and services, particular expertise may support both export and some investment activity by firms with distinctive goods supported by proprietary rights. These are the now-famous niche fillers. Canada's role in this area is exemplified by telecommunications specialists and software companies. Both export and some marketing and servicing outlets in external markets may be possible.

While trade is possible in all the above categories, investment prospects will depend more on the type of product concerned, and will be strongest for Canada in resource-based products — including some with specialized characteristics based on technology, marketing, and servicing. Apart from the resource-based sectors, much depends on how effectively Canadian firms choose their specialties and maintain their ability to innovate.

# 4

# Canada's Economic
# Strategy in the Pacific

For nearly a century, Canadian economic development emphasized infrastructure and protection — the building of transport facilities and infant-industry tariffs that were supposed to enable it to develop its industries, to support the production and export of primary products, and to limit competition from imported manufacturing.

By the early 1960s, it was realized that the Canadian market was large enough so that protection of secondary industry was no longer necessary for the preservation of manufacturing. The basic strategy gradually changed to a combination of rationalization of secondary industry and reduction of tariff and nontariff barriers to trade. This object was pursued by multilateral and bilateral means. The Kennedy and Tokyo Rounds of negotiations under the General Agreement on Tariffs and Trade (GATT) in the 1960s and 1970s reflected this shift — at first cautiously, and then with more emphasis on exposing protected industries to increased import competition.

In 1965, a major bilateral initiative was introduced, in the form of the Canada-U.S. Automotive Products Agreement (commonly referred to as the "auto pact"). This took a distinctive path in that it involved a bilateral commitment to eliminate tariffs affecting automobiles and original equipment parts, accompanied by a commitment by the major producers (all owned in the United States) to rationalize their operations — specializing their production operations in each country and trading automobiles and parts both ways. What this signified was that so long as tariffs existed, the individual manufacturers had little incentive to specialize their Canadian production facilities to achieve economies of scale at the plant level. Now, with the opportunity to specialize and trade, they could reduce costs, and they agreed to do so in exchange for the bilateral governmental agreement to eliminate tariffs affecting imports and exports by manufacturers.

There had always been plenty of foreign investment funds available to Canada, but it had not been efficiently used in industries where there were too many producers to permit each one to achieve economies of scale. The rationalization that had occurred in the auto sector by the late 1960s encouraged an examination of strategies in other sectors; in the 1970s, some moves along the same or comparable lines were proposed and attempted. During the 1970s, however, prices of primary products increased, especially in the food and energy sectors, and the value of the Canadian dollar also rose. As a result, investment was diverted from manufacturing and the international competitiveness of the sector declined.

The Tokyo Round of GATT negotiations, which concluded in 1979, left manufacturing industries further exposed to competition, and the success of East Asian industries — notably the Japanese auto sector, which was producing reliable, energy-efficient cars — captured an increasing share of the North American market.

By the mid-1980s, it was realized that the full rationalization of Canadian manufacturing might not be possible either by other sectoral deals such as the auto pact or by another round of multilateral negotiations. The former approach was incompatible with GATT rules in any case, and a new round of multilateral talks would have to deal with nontariff barriers that might not be as easily reduced in negotiations involving nearly 100 participants.

Canada thus moved toward an explicit acceptance of a "two-track" commercial policy, encouraged by the recommendations of the Royal Commission on the Economic Union and Development Prospects for Canada (the Macdonald Commission). This constituted a recognition of the necessity of reducing trade barriers globally, while at the same time attempting to go beyond what is possible multilaterally by seeking secure access to the markets of the country's most important trading partner. In the particular circumstances of the 1980s, the United States — whose leading role in international economic matters had declined relatively with the growth in the strength of fully reconstructed postwar Europe and Japan — had been experiencing a persistent balance-of-payments problem and seemed unable to adopt those domestic measures needed to remedy the situation. Thus, there was an understandable concern in Canada that the forces of protectionism voiced so stridently by some U.S. congressmen and sensationalist journalists would undermine the efforts of the Reagan administration to achieve a truly successful GATT round, or at least one that could accomplish as much for Canada as a bilateral deal.

The Canada-U.S. Free Trade Agreement (FTA) that was signed late in 1988 was fully compatible with GATT Article XXIV, which permits free trade arrangements that cover substantially all trade. However, it poses the question as to whether it discriminates against the interests of other important trading partners. This is particularly important for the Pacific countries, since, unlike the European Community, they are not organized into a full regional trading group — although there are two sub-regional groups with free or preferential trade agreements: Australia and New Zealand, and the Association of Southeast Asian Nations (ASEAN). To date, there has been little concern expressed over discriminatory effects of the Canada-U.S. FTA on Pacific partners, but the outcome of the Uruguay Round and its aftermath could result in new concerns along these lines.

Much of the debate about multilateralism versus regionalism can be set aside if one views the two as complementary. For students of Pacific cooperation, the issue is how to make the process both constructive and complementary to other regional initiatives. Each country is likely to make this judgment on grounds relating to its own geographic, economic, and other interests.

Canada, according to the federal government, has three main regional links: the North American, the European, and the Pacific. Canada's greatest economic interests lie in the Western Hemisphere — a relationship that now encompasses not only the United States, but, increasingly, Mexico and perhaps other countries of Latin America as well. Europe is a partner or group of partners primarily in bilateral trade and investment activity, and of fellow members in multilateral and quasi-multilateral institutions such as the GATT and the Organisation for Economic Co-operation and Development (OECD). The welding together of a new Europe as a consequence of developments in Eastern Europe offers Canada a chance to play a supportive role, but not one in which it has many advantages relative to the leading Western European powers, and no role to play in the new formal institutions that are likely to emerge there.

The Pacific is a different story. Here, Canada has an opportunity to play a significant role, and one that is on equal terms with other members. It may offer the particularly attractive option of building a wider and more influential, though looser, community of developing and developed countries — including those of the Americas, East Asia, and Australasia. The dynamics of the area may also assist the Soviet Union to strengthen the economic basis of *perestroika*, in part by supplying capital and technology to Siberian development projects. None of this should, however, be pursued as a countermeasure against the new Europe. If that occurs, it will constitute a failure of both multilateral and regional strategies.

The aim of a Pacific-oriented priority is to deal with the problems and opportunities of the region in a way that is fully compatible with the existence of continued and improved trade and other economic relations with Europe and, specifically, in ways conducive to even better results in multilateral institutions. Consensus building in the Pacific will be conducive to such an outcome if it satisfies three main objectives:

- if it recognizes the interests of all five non-European OECD countries (Australia, Canada, Japan, New Zealand, and the United States);
- if it can be a means of accommodating China and other East Asian nations, where various versions of the mixed economy seek sustainable growth by acknowledging and adjusting to the discipline and opportunity of world markets; and, probably most important,
- if it becomes the first economic policy consultative and "issue-alliance" group that genuinely treats developed and developing countries as equals. This last objective will be achieved when newly industrialized countries can pass smoothly to fully developed status by the standards used in multilateral institutions. They must also be convinced that they enjoy access to markets equal to that enjoyed among their most industrially advanced partners.

Canada's role in achieving these objectives can be a mixture of its usual postwar roles as honest broker or middle power. But it should be stressed that Canada's objective is not entirely altruistic. On the political level, its serious involvement in Pacific economic affairs could be, in part, a counterweight to the dominant and somewhat obsessive relationship with the

United States, and a more realistic approach than Trudeau's "third option". On the economic level, it could open up economic initiatives that are flexible and central to the smooth evolution of a multipolar international economic system.

## Canada's Priorities in Bilateral Relations within the Pacific Region

### *Japan*

Any discussion of bilateral initiatives and related unilateral Canadian moves in the Pacific must start with Japan — Canada's most important trading partner in the region, after the United States. The recent surge in Japanese investment interest in Canada has been related, in part, to the Canada-U.S. FTA, and it is vital that Canada continue to encourage this investment, and the growth of Canadian-Japanese trade, through every means that is compatible with the FTA.

For Japan, the most serious issue arising out of the FTA is the role of Japanese auto manufacturers in North American automobile and parts production. In particular, the FTA sets up newly defined content requirements for vehicles traded within North America — 50 percent of direct costs, excluding overheads must now be Canadian or U.S. in origin — and requires that Canada end its practice of providing duty remissions on offshore parts, a practice from which Japanese producers have benefited.

The former means that Japanese producers will have to source a high proportion of their components in either Canada or the United States so that their automobile products can pass duty free across the Canada-U.S. border. The latter is a rather more complex issue. Canada could, in effect, compensate Japanese producers for the ending of duty remissions by reducing its tariffs on offshore parts to the same level as that imposed by the United States. The level of Canadian duties on auto components from overseas is about 9 percent, about three times the level of U.S. duties. There is a strong case for reducing these to the U.S. level so that there is no disincentive on this account to the production of Japanese vehicles in Canada. It has been argued that, in return for this "concession", the Japanese ought to make some parallel tariff concession. This seems highly questionable, since Canada should be compensating the Japanese for the new discrimination introduced by the FTA.[1] It is also in Canada's interest to encourage North American producers to engage in joint ventures with these same producers so as to satisfy the requirements of continental or overseas competitiveness.

While pursuing its bilateral relations with Japan, Canada will have to keep a close watch on the development of U.S.-Japanese trade links. Leading figures of the Bush administration, including Secretary of State James Baker, have indicated their wish to explore a bilateral trade deal with Japan. It is rather unlikely that such a deal would soon result in the kind of comprehensive arrangement that exists between Canada and the United States. Nevertheless, the Japanese and Americans could identify common ground on a number of nontariff trade issues. If it is not to be left out, Canada should conduct parallel explorations with the Japanese on any of these issues that affect us — including, for example, the service sector, subsidies and countervailing duties, and intellectual-property rights. Once such areas have been identified as the locus of a possible agreement, Canada could fruitfully conduct bilateral discussions along the same lines with smaller Pacific partners — South Korea, Australia, and New Zealand, for example — so that the interests of the "lesser economic powers" will be reflected in proposals for an agreement between the Pacific superpowers. Fundamentally, this calls for flexibility, and for

---

1 In a recent newspaper report, it was stated that Japanese companies expect to be able to achieve 60 percent North American content by the criterion noted above.

a more rapid and constructive, rather than reactive, response to the bilateral initiative of the Pacific superpowers.


## South Korea

Canada's dealings with South Korea have been largely reactive in the past. There has, in fact, been much to react to, since South Korea has repeatedly shown its inclination to give preferential treatment to U.S. exports at the expense of those from Canada — an inclination not entirely voluntary given South Korea's dependence on the United States for its military security. Canadian business has made plenty of effort to sell in South Korea, but there has been much less government-to-government effort to work jointly on issues where a packaging of mutual interests might be beneficial. Recent developments suggesting closer South Korean economic relations with China and the Soviet Union could offer Canada the chance to become a joint venture partner involving South Korea as a market for raw materials, its larger communist neighbors as suppliers, and Canadians as providers of capital and technology in those areas where Canadian comparative advantages clearly exist. In the short run, the exploration of specific-issue alliances in trans-Pacific trade negotiations could also bring South Korea and Canada together. Hyundai, as an investor in Canadian automotive production should, of course, be accorded benefits similar to those for Japanese firms.

Most fundamental to the identification of Canada's economic interests with both South Korea and Japan is to remedy Canadians' serious lack of expertise on these two countries. Canadians, particularly at a cultural level, tend to pay much more attention to China and Southeast Asia than to their two largest trading partners in East Asia. For a country that has so many pretensions of internationalism, the superficiality of Canadian knowledge of these ancient cultures and dynamic modern economies and the virtual neglect of Japanese and

Korean language training is shortsighted, to say the least. It leaves Canada at a distinct disadvantage not only relative to its U.S. competitors but also to those from Australia, whose government has in place a well-financed program of studies on its Western Pacific neighbors at its federally financed Research School of Pacific Studies at the Australian National University.

## Australia and New Zealand

In the case of Australia and New Zealand, these two Commonwealth countries have already established a Closer Economic Relations (CER) arrangement that goes beyond a free trade area to a partial economic union with a large measure of factor mobility and some policy harmonization. A recent study commissioned by the New Zealand government examined the merits of a similar arrangement between the CER members and Canada.[2] The study concluded that regionalism might benefit from a "stepping-stone" approach, which would bring together more quickly those countries with the most in common. This would not preclude participation of the three countries in geographically or economically limited arrangements — for example, codes on nontariff barriers — open to participation by other members.

The reaction in Canada to the New Zealand proposal has been cautious, in good part because of Canadians' current preoccupation with the Canada-U.S. FTA. Another reason for caution is that Australia and New Zealand have a combined gross national product that is one-half that of Canada, and all three countries are substantially dependent on natural-resource-based exports. Although there is considerable variety

2 See Frank Holmes, ed., *Stepping Stones to Freer Trade?* (Wellington, New Zealand: Victoria University Press, 1989). On the more general question of future free trade areas in the Pacific, involving the United States, see Jeffrey Schott, ed., *More Free Trade Areas?* (Washington, D.C.: Institute for International Economics, 1989).

in their patterns of such exports, and although Canada already exports a variety of manufactures to Australia and New Zealand, the trade potential from such an arrangement cannot be compared to that with the United States. For analogous reasons, Australian commentators also have been skeptical about the value of free trade among the three countries.

## The Rest of the Pacific Region

The success of these bilateral initiatives will depend on how they accommodate the interests of the newly industrialized economies (Hong Kong, South Korea, and Taiwan), China, and the ASEAN group. Here, the challenge will be to find middle ground between "special and differential status" and "graduation" — ground that will, moreover, be different from country to country and from group to group. It has been suggested that countries with higher than a specified level of gross domestic product per capita should be expected to bind tariffs at lower rates.

Whatever the choice of means, these countries will have to gain market access for products of prime interest to them if they are to consider themselves equal beneficiaries of any Pacific initiatives. It is noteworthy that the spread of possible free trade arrangements among the developed countries of the Pacific significantly reduces the meaning of "special and differential status" — and especially the meaning of the generalized system of preferences. This poses a special challenge to the developed countries of the region. Whatever its form, the only meaningful guideline available to the developed countries is to place the highest priority on the reduction of tariff and nontariff barriers affecting those products and services in which developing countries have the greatest comparative advantages. In order to ensure that developed countries will pay appropriate attention to this initiative, the developing countries, while retaining infant-industry protection to support their future specialties, might well consider restructuring their tariffs to avoid the diversion of resources into areas of low advantage for them. They might even offer to make modest reductions in tariffs and nontariff barriers and even binding of existing tariff levels in response to commitments by the developed countries to substantial new access to their markets. Such "limited reciprocity" could thus enhance the developing countries leverage in their regional and multilateral dealings.[3] The newly industrialized countries might be expected to go further in this direction than their less-developed neighbors.

## A Trade Policy Package for the Pacific

In this concluding section, the scope for Pacific cooperation is illustrated by a package of trade policy proposals that the countries of the Pacific region might consider implementing to their collective advantage. This is followed by a few comments on the implications for Canada's domestic policy priorities of its participating in such a regional trading initiative.

It should be stressed that a balanced selection of the following specific proposals should be adopted concurrently, so that the varied priorities of the region can be served:

- (i) an agreement on the substantial reduction or removal of trade barriers on all tropical products in raw and processed form, particularly for those mainly supplied by Pacific Rim countries;
- (ii) an agreement on the substantial reduction of trade barriers affecting temperate-zone natural products and processed forms of those products, conditional only on a reasonable period of adjustment for selected products — such as rice — crucial to security of supply;

3 Note the statements by representatives from South Korea, the Philippines, and Indonesia in H.E. English, ed., *Pacific Initiatives in Global Trade* (Halifax: Institute for Research on Public Policy, 1990), pp. 316–323, 325–329.

- (iii) over a reasonable period, a substantial reduction or elimination of trade barriers affecting labor-intensive manufactures — in particular, the phased elimination of non-tariff barriers, especially on textile products; but an immediate collective commitment by the developed countries to raise the minimum annual percentage increase of such imports, probably by expanding quotas;
- (iv) a more comprehensive and precise definition of "countervailable subsidies" and of "appropriate countervail action", and a move toward a more economically meaningful administration of antidumping measures;
- (v) an umbrella agreement on the principles for liberalizing trade in services, and moves to apply those principles to a group of sectors, including some of interest to each group of countries in the Pacific region — for example, some or all of financial services, commercial aviation and tourism, construction services, and engineering services;
- (vi) an agreement to govern the practices and policies affecting trade in goods (and services) to which intellectual-property rights apply — in particular, with a view to controlling "counterfeit trade"; and
- (vii) guidelines for the more complete participation of Pacific countries in the GATT, with special reference to China and Taiwan — noting and, where appropriate, applying the Hong Kong precedent, which permits the city state to have a separate membership in the GATT because it has a separate customs system.

The packaging of these proposals could be comprehensive or more selective. For example, it is likely that (i) and (ii) might be combined, as they embody the interests of all major raw material exporters — 11 of the 14 larger members of the Pacific Economic Cooperation Conference (PECC) group would be served by this. A package covering manufactures and services incorporating (iii) to (vi) could serve interests in virtually all Pacific region countries.

These ideas are applicable to the further development of specific-issue alliances in multilateral trade negotiations. They are equally applicable to regional initiatives compatible with the GATT. All arrangements emerging from these processes should be open to other countries, which could then lay the foundation for the Pacific Rim Latin American countries to participate or to form parallel arrangements using a similar form and content.

Canada's active support for many of these Pacific basin initiatives should provide an expanding basis for national prosperity based on an internationally competitive economy. It is clear, however, that Canadian domestic policies will need to undergo a thorough re-examination at both the federal and provincial levels if the country is to respond to the new Pacific challenges and opportunities. The kind of policy changes required are likely to include the following:

- a strengthening of scientific, engineering and commercial, and education services;
- the appropriate adjustment of R&D incentive systems, probably emphasizing general tax credits;
- appropriate policies to support sustainable development of renewable natural resources;
- rationalization of the tax system so as to reduce the distortion of taxes that discriminate against export competitiveness — the goods and services tax was directed to this objective, but it has been encumbered by the failure of federal-provincial cooperation and much political static;
- a social safety net that operates efficiently — that is, one that comprises at least the present level of income support, but that also combines some programs so as to remove the risks of sectoral distortions to the fullest extent possible,

particularly in heavily protected sectors such as supply-
managed agriculture and textile products; and
• coordination of federal and provincial policies so that efforts
to support particular sectors do not obstruct emerging,
dynamic comparative advantages.

Above all, Canadians must be willing to adjust. This means
acceptance of new industries or new leaders in established
industries, with ample provision for those who will bear the
main burden of adjustment, especially workers. It is encouraging to observe acknowledgment that low-wage, labor-intensive sectors — some parts of the textile products industry in
Quebec, for example — will have to be allowed to decline and
that new manufacturing opportunities will have to be found in
more skill- or technology-intensive sectors. The Canada-U.S.
FTA is perceived as contributing significantly to this objective,
but adjustment has clearly been hampered by high interest
rates and the higher value of the Canadian dollar.

A Canadian economy that is more fully and coherently
oriented toward the challenges and opportunities of the Pacific
will also be one that is ready and able to compete successfully
in the wider world marketplace.

Pacific economic cooperation serves this objective in many
specific ways. The Pacific generally serves Canada's trade
objectives: as a reliable and expanding market for resource
products in the richer, but resource-deficient, countries of
Northeast Asia; as an outlet for selected technology-intensive
products relevant to resource development in China, Southeast
Asia, and the South Pacific; and as a market for Canadian
transport and communications products and services in many
of these economies.

Outside the trade field, technology exchange across the
Pacific will certainly be central to Canada-Japan linkages, and
should foster foreign direct investment inflow from Japan as
well as other institutional cooperation in the applied sciences.
As for commercial and financial linkages, major opportunities

are likely to focus on Hong Kong, Singapore, and Taiwan, assisted by Canada's growing Chinese business community.

Cooperation in policy harmonization, as well as the evolution of emerging international institutions such as PECC and APEC (Asia Pacific Economic Cooperation), probably should stress the combined efforts of Canada with the smaller powers — South Korea, the ASEAN countries, Australia, and New Zealand. Together, these countries can build consensus positions that the superpowers of the region should find attractive and perhaps compelling.

## *Recent Developments:*
## *Two Blocs or one Partnership?*

As urgent negotiations continue in an effort to avoid under-achievment in the Uruguay Round of GATT negotiations, some disturbing alternative strategies by major economic powers are beginning to emerge. The prospect of a three-bloc world — a Europe led by Germany, a Western hemisphere led by the United States, and a Western Pacific group led by Japan — is receiving increased currency in the business press.

The implication of the conflict in the Persian Gulf for rivalry among the three economic superpowers is not yet being addressed, but it raises the key question: Will the scope for Pacific cooperation be undermined by the combined effect of the shortfall of results from the Uruguay Round and the economic and political costs of the rebirth of U.S. hegemony in the post–Cold War era?

The Bush administration has made it clear that, in trade and other international relations, it intends to apply the "hub-and-spoke" principle, as exemplified by its decision to negotiate a bilateral free trade arrangement with Mexico — which is sometimes represented as a logical follow-up to the Canada-U.S. FTA. But the Bush administration has moved beyond this, indicating a plan for similar bilateral negotiations with other

Latin American countries, with a view ultimately to achieving a hemispheric economic integration in some form. Informed observers in the United States have recently indicated that one of the administration's intentions — or, at least, a hoped-for implication — is to sublimate any tendency on the part of the U.S. Congress to react to the Uruguay Round shortfall by moving to more protectionist-oriented bilateralism.

It is not at all clear that Western Hemisphere deals would be effective in preventing the Pacific from becoming an arena of economic conflict. According to recent reports from official sources, the idea of hub-and-spoke arrangements may also be applied in the Pacific. Under a different name, this idea was proposed some years ago by then U.S. Trade Representative William Brock. U.S.-South Korea, U.S.-Taiwan, and U.S.-ASEAN deals were cited as possibilities. Mike Mansfield, former U.S. ambassador to Japan, suggested a U.S.-Japan arrangement, although the hub-and-spoke label clearly would not be appropriate in this case.

The important issue is whether Congress would be prepared to accommodate East Asian competition with the same equanimity it might evidence in Western Hemisphere deals. Americans, and many U.S. business sectors, have become very sensitive to the fact that their toughest competition comes from East Asia. Moreover, too many are also convinced that the strength of their East Asian rivals is based on "unfair" forms of competition, requiring tough bargaining and even threats such as those associated with super-301. Although saner U.S. views still call for strengthening that country's industrial, technological, and education base and for freeing savings for use in the civilian sector, the Gulf War makes it more doubtful that this view can prevail.[4]

---

4 In 1989, there was considerable skepticism about the feasibility of the bilateral approach, especially as it applied to Asia. See, for example, the papers presented in Jeffrey J. Schott, ed., *Free Trade Areas and U.S. Trade Policy* (Washington, D.C.: Institute for International Economics, 1989).

An approach based on issue-oriented Pacific consensus building and cooperation — one that deals with major trade and other policy challenges that remain high priorities — seems much better suited to the interests of the Pacific countries, including the United States.The combined GNP of North America and the Western Pacific exceeds US$9 trillion, compared with US$5 trillion for all of Europe (excluding the Soviet Union). The trade and investment initiatives emerging for the Pacific and open to adherence by Europe are more likely to maintain a multilateral and liberal bias in international relations.

Because of this, and also because of its unique position as the largest and closest economic partner of the United States, Canada has both a national interest and a political opportunity to discourage a trend toward two blocs in the region and to provide a constructive contribution to the Pacific partnership option.

One reason for this is Canada's special role in the first hub-and-spoke deal with Mexico. Here, Canada's first aim will be to protect its interests in the FTA. Only slightly less important is Canada's historic concern to conduct bilateral relations with the United States in a larger context. The 1991 form of any initiative serving this objective would seek to ensure that any North American arrangement does not discriminate in any significant way against Asian suppliers of labor-intensive goods, or against investment from Japan.

Another reason would be to address the major nontariff barriers that remain in place through proposals that invite the participation of all Pacific countries, and are open to adherence by others as well. Mexico should also be interested in this kind of initiative, both because it is now a member of PECC and because, like Canada, it prefers to view negotiations in North America not as substitutes but as complements to wider initiatives.

Canada's commitment to these objectives should be reinforced at this time, and not be sidetracked by short-term political preoccupations. It must be admitted here, however, that there is a substantial risk at present that the Pacific will be treated as entirely tomorrow's priority.

*Appendix Tables*

## Table A-1
### Factors Affecting the Economic Performance of Selected Pacific Economies

| Countries (ranked by GDP size in groups) | Population growth rates (%) | | Urban population (%) | Investment (% of GDP) | | Export shares (% of GDP) | |
|---|---|---|---|---|---|---|---|
| | 1960–65 | 1985–90[a] | | 1970 | 1987 | 1970 | 1987 |
| *Most developed* | | | | | | | |
| United States | 1.5 | 0.8 | 74 | 18 | 18 | 6 | 8 |
| Japan | 1.0 | 0.4 | 77 | 34 | 28 | 11 | 13 |
| Canada | 1.8 | 1.1 | 75 | 22 | 21 | 23 | 26 |
| Australia | 2.0 | 1.2 | 87 | 27 | 24 | 15 | 16 |
| New Zealand | 2.0 | 0.8 | 84 | 24 | 25 | 22 | 28 |
| *East Asia* | | | | | | | |
| China | 1.8 | 1.0 | 21 | 36[c] | 46 | 3 | 14 |
| South Korea | 2.6 | 1.4 | 65 | 25 | 29 | 14 | 45 |
| Taiwan | 3.3[b] | 1.9 | n/a | 26 | 20 | 30 | 61 |
| Hong Kong | 3.6 | 1.8 | 91 | 21 | 26 | 93 | 126 |

## Table A-1 - continued

| Countries (ranked by GDP size in groups) | Population growth rates (%) | | Urban population (%) | Investment (% of GDP) | | Export shares (% of GDP) | |
|---|---|---|---|---|---|---|---|
| | 1960–65 | 1985–90[a] | | 1970 | 1987 | 1970 | 1987 |
| *Southeast Asia* | | | | | | | |
| Indonesia | 2.1 | 1.6 | 25 | 14 | 26 | 13 | 21 |
| Thailand | 3.0 | 1.7 | 16 | 26 | 21 | 14 | 45 |
| Philippines | 3.0 | 2.3 | 40 | 21 | 15 | 19 | 23 |
| Malaysia | 3.0 | 2.2 | 32 | 20 | 24 | 40 | 57 |
| Singapore | 2.8 | 1.2 | 74 | 39 | 39 | 82 | 129 |
| *Pacific Islands* | | | | | | | |
| Papua-New Guinea | 2.6 | 1.8 | 14 | 47 | 24 | 19 | 45 |
| Fiji | 3.3 | 1.5 | 41 | 22 | 17 | 48 | 44 |

[a] Based on United Nations projections.

[b] 1958–66 basis.

[c] Chinese figures include Taiwan.

Source: *Asia-Pacific Report* (Honolulu: East-West Center, 1989), appendix tables.

## Table A-2

### *Canada's Bilateral Trade with Selected Pacific Countries: An Overview of the 1980s*

(C$ millions)

|  | 1980 | 1982 | 1985 | 1986 | 1987 | 1988 |
|---|---|---|---|---|---|---|
| **United States** | | | | | | |
| Exports (to) | $48,174 | $57,685 | $93,059 | $93,206 | $94,506 | $101,008 |
| Imports (from) | 47,446 | 46,907 | 72,020 | 75,228 | 76,716 | 86,509 |
| Balance | 728 | 10,778 | 21,039 | 17,979 | 17,790 | 14,499 |
| **Japan** | | | | | | |
| Exports | 4,374 | 4,590 | 5,757 | 5,968 | 7,074 | 8,727 |
| Imports | 2,904 | 3,711 | 6,731 | 8,367 | 8,351 | 9,265 |
| Balance | 1,469 | 879 | (994) | (2,400) | (1,277) | (538) |
| **Australia** | | | | | | |
| Exports | 679 | 698 | 676 | 653 | 702 | 894 |
| Imports | 521 | 448 | 365 | 498 | 563 | 672 |
| Balance | 157 | 255 | 311 | 155 | 140 | 221 |
| **New Zealand** | | | | | | |
| Exports | 115 | 159 | 193 | 152 | 140 | 143 |
| Imports | 151 | 145 | 162 | 181 | 220 | 225 |
| Balance | (36) | 14 | 31 | (29) | (80) | (83) |
| **China** | | | | | | |
| Exports | 874 | 1,232 | 1,297 | 1,124 | 1,438 | 2,603 |
| Imports | 182 | 264 | 438 | 594 | 812 | 955 |
| Balance | 692 | 968 | 858 | 530 | 625 | 1,648 |
| **South Korea** | | | | | | |
| Exports | 512 | 488 | 786 | 975 | 1,178 | 1,209 |
| Imports | 433 | 603 | 1,652 | 1,798 | 1,912 | 2,271 |
| Balance | 80 | 9115) | (866) | (824) | (735) | 1,062 |
| **Taiwan** | | | | | | |
| Exports | 254 | 305 | 434 | 616 | 766 | 996 |
| Imports | 579 | 695 | 1,378 | 1,877 | 2,166 | 2,257 |
| Balance | (325) | (390) | (944) | (1,261) | (1,400) | (1,261) |
| **Hong Kong** | | | | | | |
| Exports | 199 | 265 | 346 | 333 | 491 | 1,004 |
| Imports | 557 | 627 | 852 | 1,003 | 1,098 | 1,153 |
| Balance | (358) | (362) | (506) | (559) | (607) | (149) |

## Table A-2 - continued

|  | 1980 | 1982 | 1985 | 1986 | 1987 | 1988 |
|---|---|---|---|---|---|---|
| **Indonesia** |  |  |  |  |  |  |
| Exports | 216 | 208 | 259 | 255 | 310 | 318 |
| Imports | 77 | 57 | 122 | 142 | 193 | 179 |
| Balance | 138 | 151 | 136 | 113 | 116 | 139 |
| **Thailand** |  |  |  |  |  |  |
| Exports | 142 | 146 | 133 | 112 | 201 | 267 |
| Imports | 39 | 46 | 122 | 161 | 210 | 344 |
| Balance | 103 | 101 | 10 | (50) | (9) | (77) |
| **Philippines** |  |  |  |  |  |  |
| Exports | 86 | 102 | 46 | 50 | 123 | 134 |
| Imports | 114 | 91 | 126 | 134 | 133 | 178 |
| Balance | (28) | 11 | (79) | (84) | (10) | (44) |
| **Malaysia** |  |  |  |  |  |  |
| Exports | 95 | 125 | 209 | 109 | 121 | 184 |
| Imports | 167 | 124 | 204 | 208 | 257 | 324 |
| Balance | (71) | 1 | 5 | (100) | (136) | (140) |
| **Singapore** |  |  |  |  |  |  |
| Exports | 202 | 155 | 120 | 155 | 178 | 294 |
| Imports | 105 | 102 | 186 | 208 | 291 | 466 |
| Balance | 97 | 53 | (66) | (53) | (113) | (172) |
| **All PECC (except U.S.)** |  |  |  |  |  |  |
| Exports | 7,747 | 8,473 | 10,235 | 10,500 | 12,721 | 16,773 |
| Imports | 5,828 | 6,907 | 12,339 | 15,172 | 16,208 | 18,291 |
| Balance | 1,919 | 1,565 | (2,103) | (4,671) | (3,486) | (1,518) |
| **Western Europe** |  |  |  |  |  |  |
| Exports | 11,292 | 8,770 | 8,191 | 9,252 | 10,788 | 12,861 |
| Imports | 7,069 | 7,133 | 12,752 | 15,046 | 16,134 | 18,890 |
| Balance | 4,223 | 1,638 | (4,562) | (5,794) | (5,346) | (6,029) |
| **Eastern Europe** |  |  |  |  |  |  |
| Exports | 2,148 | 2,590 | 1,910 | 1,614 | 1,013 | 1,401 |
| Imports | 331 | 260 | 325 | 366 | 418 | 614 |
| Balance | 1,817 | 2,330 | 1,585 | 1,248 | 595 | 787 |
| *World total* |  |  |  |  |  |  |
| *Exports* | *76,159* | *84,530* | *119,475* | *120,670* | *125,087* | *138,150* |
| *Imports* | *69,274* | *67,856* | *104,355* | *112,511* | *116,239* | *131,664* |
| *Balance* | *6,885* | *16,675* | *15,119* | *8,158* | *8,848* | *6,486* |

Source: Department of External Affairs, based on data from Statistics Canada.

**Table A-3**

*Canada's Leading Groups of Exports and Imports, Selected Pacific Countries, 1988*

(C$ millions)

| Exports | | Imports | |
|---|---|---|---|
| **United States** | | | |
| Vehicles and parts | 32,066 | Vehicles and parts | 24,312 |
| Pulp and paper | 10,248 | Nonelectrical machinery and equipment | 17,605 |
| Mineral fuels | 10,152 | Electrical machinery and equipment | 8,034 |
| Nonelectrical machinery and equipment | 8,262 | Plastics and products | 2,630 |
| Wood products | 4,653 | Precision equipment | 2,469 |
| *Total exports* | *97,842* | *Total imports* | *86,449* |
| **Japan** | | | |
| Mineral fuels | 1,482 | Vehicles and parts | 3,240 |
| Wood products | 1,182 | Nonelectrical machinery and equipment | 1,985 |
| Pulp | 946 | Electrical machinery and equipment | 1,837 |
| Ores | 855 | Precision equipment | 480 |
| Oilseeds and products | 657 | Iron and steel products | 240 |
| Fish | 583 | | |
| *Total exports* | *8,680* | *Total imports* | *9,254* |

## Table A-3 - continued

| Exports | | Imports | |
|---|---|---|---|
| **Australia** | | | |
| Pulp and paper | 175 | Inorganic chemicals | 201 |
| Wood products | 106 | Sugar and products | 122 |
| Nonelectrical machinery and equipment | 89 | Meat | 120 |
| Nonmetallic minerals | 64 | Plant products | 29 |
| Vehicles and parts | 60 | Nonelectrical machinery and equipment | 27 |
| Plastics and products | 47 | | |
| *Total exports* | *842* | *Total imports* | *663* |
| **New Zealand** | | | |
| Nonelectrical machinery and equipment | 21 | Meat | 111 |
| Nonmetallic minerals | 15 | Fruit | 26 |
| Plastics and products | 15 | Dairy products | 11 |
| Paper products | 11 | Iron and steel | 8 |
| Electrical machinery and equipment | 10 | Hides and leather | 8 |
| Fish | 9 | | |
| *Total exports* | *138* | *Total imports* | *225* |

## Table A-3 - continued

| Exports | | Imports | |
|---|---|---|---|
| **China** | | | |
| Cereals | 1,679 | Apparel | 206 |
| Plastics and products | 230 | Toys and sports goods | 96 |
| Pulp and paper | 225 | Leather products (except footwear) | 80 |
| Fertilizers | 161 | Electrical equipment | 74 |
| Nonelectrical machinery and equipment | 59 | Footwear | 44 |
| *Total exports* | 2,593 | *Total imports* | 955 |
| **South Korea** | | | |
| Mineral fuels | 242 | Electrical equipment | 513 |
| Pulp | 142 | Apparel | 207 |
| Organic chemicals | 140 | Vehicles and parts | 194 |
| Aluminum and products | 96 | Nonelectrical machinery and equipment | 193 |
| Ores | 84 | Footwear | 142 |
| *Total exports* | 1,200 | *Total imports* | 2,272 |

## Table A-3 - continued

### Taiwan

| Exports | | Imports | |
|---|---|---|---|
| Pulp and paper | 129 | Nonelectrical machinery and equipment | 364 |
| Organic chemicals | 98 | Electrical equipment | 323 |
| Hides and leather | 93 | Apparel | 251 |
| Mineral fuels | 90 | Footwear | 152 |
| Aluminum and products | 51 | Furniture (including bedding) | 136 |
| | | Vehicles and parts | 134 |
| *Total exports* | 967 | *Total imports* | 2,258 |

### Hong Kong

| Exports | | Imports | |
|---|---|---|---|
| Precious stones and metals | 432 | Apparel | 413 |
| Pulp and paper | 83 | Electrical equipment | 176 |
| Plastics and products | 46 | Toys and sports equipment | 70 |
| Aluminum and products | 45 | Clocks and watches | 58 |
| Electrical machinery and equipment | 41 | Cotton | 33 |
| *Total exports* | 986 | *Total imports* | 1,155 |

## Table A-3 - continued

| Exports | | Imports | |
|---|---|---|---|
| **Indonesia** | | | |
| Pulp and paper | 67 | Rubber and products | 60 |
| Cereals | 56 | Wood and products | 50 |
| Plastics and products | 47 | Apparel | 27 |
| Nonmetallic minerals | 32 | Coffee, tea, and spices | 12 |
| Fertilizers | 31 | Man-made staple fibres | 6 |
| *Total exports* | *299* | *Total imports* | *180* |
| **Malaysia** | | | |
| Fertilizers | 41 | Electrical equipment | 149 |
| Paper products | 27 | Rubber and products | 62 |
| Aluminum and products | 14 | Apparel | 29 |
| Animal and vegetable fats and oils | 14 | Animal and vegetable fats and oils | 24 |
| Cereals | 12 | Meat and fish products | 14 |
| *Total exports* | *192* | *Total imports* | *324* |

## Table A-3 - continued

| Exports | | Imports | |
|---|---|---|---|
| **Philippines** | | | |
| Fertilizers | 23 | Apparel | 46 |
| Paper products | 16 | Electrical equipment | 33 |
| Plastics and products | 12 | Plant products | 11 |
| Cereals | 10 | Meat and fish products | 10 |
| Dairy and other edible products | 9 | Clocks and watches | 9 |
| *Total exports* | *131* | *Total imports* | *178* |
| **Singapore** | | | |
| Precious stones and metals | 36 | Nonelectrical machinery and equipment | 216 |
| Paper products | 36 | Electrical machinery and equipment | 153 |
| Electrical machinery and equipment | 32 | Apparel | 21 |
| Fertilizers | 23 | Organic chemicals | 15 |
| Nonelectrical machinery and equipment | 23 | Toys and sports equipment | 10 |
| *Total exports* | *275* | *Total imports* | *467* |

## Table A-3 - continued

### Thailand

| Exports | | Imports | |
|---------|---|---------|---|
| Pulp and paper | 43 | Vehicles and parts | 74 |
| Aluminum and products | 40 | Meat and fish products | 68 |
| Nonmetallic minerals | 32 | Apparel | 41 |
| Iron and steel | 31 | Plant products | 21 |
| Nonelectrical machinery and equipment | 19 | Nonelectrical machinery and equipment | 11 |
| Total exports | 259 | Total imports | 343 |

Note:   Some of the totals in this table do not correspond to those in Table A-2, since Table A-3 was prepared at a time when the data were in a preliminary form for 1988.

Source:   Department of External Affairs.

## Table A-4

### Canada's External Assistance Program to Western Pacific Economies, fiscal years 1985–86 to 1987–88

(C$ millions)

|  | 1985–86 | 1986–87 | 1987–88 |
|---|---|---|---|
| China | $15.5 | $27.0 | $35.3 |
| Indonesia | 74.9 | 42.0 | 44.4 |
| Malaysia | 1.0 | 1.8 | 1.8 |
| Philippines | 0.5 | 9.7 | 22.1 |
| Thailand | 8.6 | 22.0 | 29.4 |
| Total | 100.5 | 102.5 | 133.0 |
| Pacific islands | 1.5 | 1.3 | 2.4 |
| Total bilateral aid | 816.2 | 967.0 | 1,101.2 |
| Asian Development Bank | 91.9 | 139.6 | 73.2 |

Source: Canadian International Development Agency.

# Selected Bibliography
## on Pacific Institutions *

Akrasanee, Narongchai, Seiji Naya, and Vinyu Vichit-Vadakan (eds.). *Trade and Employment in Asia and the Pacific.* Honolulu: University of Hawaii Press, 1977.

Asia Pacific Economic Cooperation. "Joint Statement," Ministerial-Level Meeting and "Summary Statement by the Chairman," Senator Gareth Evans, Canberra, November 7, 1989.

*Asia-Pacific Report.* Honolulu: East-West Center, Annual.

*Asia Yearbook.* Hong Kong: Review Publishing Company, Annual.

Asian Development Bank. *Annual Reports.* Manila.

Australia. Department of Foreign Affairs and Trade. "Australia's Regional Economic Co-operation Initiative: An Idea Whose Time Has Come." Address by Senator Gareth Evans, Minister for Foreign Affairs and Trade, at the Opening of the Twelfth Australia-ASEAN Forum, Perth, May 15, 1989.

Australia. Department of the Prime Minister and Cabinet. "Regional Co-operation: Challenges for Korea and Australia." Speech by the Prime Minister to Luncheon of Korea Business Associations, Seoul, Korea, January 31, 1989.

Australia. Minister for Trade Negotiations. "Asia-Pacific Economic Co-operation Challenges and Options for Australia." News Release No. MN4 (Address by Minister for Trade Negotiations and Acting Minister for Foreign Affairs and Trade, Mr. Duffy, to CEDA), February 9, 1989.

Bautista, Romeo M., and Seiji Naya. Eds. *Energy and Structural Change in the Asia-Pacific Region.* Manila: Philippine Institute for Development Studies and Asian Development Bank, 1984.

---

* Most of the citations in this bibliography are taken, with permission, from Lawrence T. Woods, "Diplomacy and International Nongovernmental Organizations: A Study of the Pacific Economic Cooperation Movement." Doctoral Dissertation, Australian National University, Canberra, 1988.

Boyd, Gavin. Ed. *Region Building in the Pacific.* New York: Pergamon, 1982.

———— (ed.). *Regionalism and Global Security.* Lexington, Mass.: D.C. Heath, 1984.

Bull, Hedley (ed.). *Asia and the Western Pacific: Towards a New International Order.* Sydney: Thomas Nelson; Australian Institute of International Affairs, 1975.

Canadian Chamber of Commerce. *Report of the Fifth Pacific Economic Cooperation Conference, Vancouver, November 16–19, 1986.* Ottawa, 1987.

Canadian Committee, PBEC. "Asia and the Pacific: Challenge and Opportunity for Canada." Submission to the Special Parliamentary Joint Committee on International Relations, Ottawa, December 13, 1985.

Canadian National Committee on Pacific Economic Cooperation. *Canada and the Pacific Region.* Ottawa, 1989.

Castle, Leslie V., and Frank Holmes (eds.). *Cooperation and Development in the Asia-Pacific Region — Relations Between Large and Small Countries.* Tokyo: Japan Economic Research Center, 1976.

Centre for Strategic and International Studies. *Asia-Pacific in the 1980s: Toward Greater Symmetry in Economic Interdependence.* Jakarta, 1980.

————. *Issues for Pacific Economic Cooperation: A Report of the Third Pacific Economic Cooperation Conference, Bali, November 1983.* Jakarta, 1984.

Condliffe, J.B. (ed.). *Problems of the Pacific, 1929: Proceedings of the Third Conference of the Institute of Pacific Relations, Nara and Kyoto, Japan, October 23–November 9, 1929.* Chicago: University of Chicago Press, 1930.

Crawford, John. "The Pacific Basin Cooperative Concept." Research Paper 70, Australia–Japan Economic Relations Research Project, Australia–Japan Research Centre, Research School of Pacific Studies, Australian National University, Canberra, August 1980.

————, and Greg Seow (eds.). *Pacific Economic Co-operation: Suggestions for Action.* Selangor, Indonesia: Heinemann Educational, 1981.

————, and Saburo Okita. *Australia, Japan and the Western Pacific Economic Relations: A Report to the Governments of Australia and Japan.* Canberra: Australian Government Publishing Service, 1976.

————, and Saburo Okita (eds.). *Raw Materials and Pacific Economic Integration.* Canberra: Australian National University Press, 1978.

"Directory of Pacific Basin Institutions," *Pacific Economic Cooperation* (A Newsletter of the United States National Committee for Pacific Economic Cooperation) (Fall 1988), pp. 2–7.

Drysdale, Peter (ed.). *Direct Foreign Investment in Asia and the Pacific.* Canberra: Australian National University Press, 1972.

————. *International Economic Pluralism: Economic Policy in East Asia and the Pacific.* New York: Columbia University Press, 1988.

————. "Japan and Australia in the Pacific and World Economy." Paper prepared for the 23rd Joint Meeting of the Australia-Japan Business Cooperation Committee, Sydney, October 21–22, 1985.

————. "An Organisation for Pacific Trade, Aid and Development: Regional Arrangements and the Resource Trade." Research Paper 49, Australia-Japan Economic Relations Research Project, Australia-Japan Research Centre, Research School of Pacific Studies, Australian National University, Canberra, May 1978.

————. "The Pacific Trade and Development Conference: A Brief History." Pacific Economic Papers 112, Australia-Japan Research Centre, Research School of Pacific Studies, Australian National University, Canberra, June 1984.

English, H. Edward. "Canada and Pacific Cooperation." Research Paper Series I, Pacific Basin Project No. 2, Center for Japan-U.S. Relations, International University of Japan, 1986.

———— (ed.). *Pacific Initiatives in Global Trade.* Halifax: Institute for Research on Public Policy, 1990.

————, and Anthony Scott (eds.). *Renewable Resources in the Pacific.* Ottawa: International Development Research Centre, 1982.

————, and Keith A.J. Hay (eds.). *Obstacles to Trade in the Pacific Area.* Ottawa: School of International Affairs, Carleton University, 1972.

Evans, L.T., and J.D.B. Miller (eds.). *Policy and Practice: Essays in Honour of Sir John Crawford.* Sydney: Australian National University Press, 1987.

Garnaut, Ross (ed.). *ASEAN in a Changing Pacific and World Economy.* Canberra: Australian National University Press, 1980.

Gorbachev, Mikhail. "Speech at a Ceremonial Meeting Devoted to the Presentation of the Order of Lenin to the City of Vladivostok, July 28, 1986," *Far Eastern Affairs* (Moscow) 1 (1987): 3–21.

Harris, Stuart. "Vladivostok and Australian Foreign Policy." In Ramesh Thakur and Carlyle A. Thayer (eds.). *The Soviet Union as an Asian Pacific Power: Implications of Gorbachev's 1986 Vladivostok Initiative.* Boulder, Col.: Westview Press, 1987, pp. 113–28.

Holbrooke, Richard, Roderick MacFarquhar, and Kazuo Nukazawa. *East Asia in Transition: Challenges for the Trilateral Countries.* New York: The Trilateral Commission, 1988.

Hong, Wontack, and Lawrence B. Krause (eds.). *Trade and Growth of the Advanced Developing Countries in the Pacific Basin.* Seoul: Korea Development Institute, 1981.

Japan Center for International Exchange. *The Pacific Community Concept: Views from Eight Nations.* Tokyo, 1980.

Japan Institute of International Affairs. *Review on Pacific Cooperation Activities.* Osaka, May 1988.

Japan National Committee for Pacific Economic Cooperation. *Report of the Sixth Pacific Economic Cooperation Conference, Osaka, May 17–20, 1988.* Tokyo, 1988.

Keohane, Robert O., and Joseph S. Nye, Jr. (eds.). *Transnational Relations and World Politics.* Cambridge, Mass.: Harvard University Press, 1973.

Kirby, Stuart. "Towards the Pacific Century: Economic Development in the Pacific Basin." Special Report 137, The Economist Intelligence Unit, London, March 1983.

Kojima, Kiyoshi. *Economic Cooperation in a Pacific Community.* Tokyo: Japan Institute of International Affairs, 1980.

———. *Japan and a Pacific Free Trade Area.* London, Macmillan, 1971.

——— (ed.). *Pacific Trade and Development,* 2v. Tokyo: Japan Economic Research Center, 1968–69.

——— (ed.). *Structural Adjustments in Asian-Pacific Trade,* 2v. Tokyo: Japan Economic Research Center, 1973.

———, and Miguel S. Wionczek (eds.). *Technology Transfer in Pacific Economic Development.* Tokyo: Japan Economic Research Center, 1975.

Korea Development Institute. *Pacific Economic Cooperation — Issues and Opportunities: Report of the Fourth Pacific Economic Cooperation Conference, Seoul, April 29–May 1, 1985.* Seoul, 1985.

———. *Pacific Trade Policy Cooperation: Goals and Initiatives.* Seoul, 1986.

Krause, Lawrence B., and Hugh Patrick (eds.). *Mineral Resources in the Pacific Area*. San Francisco: Federal Reserve Bank of San Francisco, 1978.

————, and Sueo Sekiguchi (eds.). *Economic Interaction in the Pacific Basin*. Washington, D.C.: The Brookings Institution, 1980.

Langdon, Frank. *The Politics of Canadian-Japanese Economic Relations, 1952–1983*. Vancouver: University of British Columbia Press, 1983.

Linder, Staffan Burenstam. *The Pacific Century: Economic and Political Consequences of Asian-Pacific Dynamism*. Stanford: Stanford University Press, 1986.

Matsumoto, Hiroshi, and Noordin Sopiee (eds.). *Into the Pacific Era: Southeast Asia and Its Place in the Pacific*. Kuala Lumpur; Tokyo: Institute of Strategic and International Studies; Association of Promotion of International Cooperation, 1986.

Moertopo, Ali. *Indonesia in Regional and International Cooperation: Principles of Implementation and Construction*. Jakarta: Centre for Strategic and International Studies, 1973.

Mutoh, Hiromichi, et al. (eds.). *Industrial Policies for Pacific Economic Growth*. Sydney: Allen and Unwin, 1986.

National Pacific Cooperation Committee of Australia. *Australia and Pacific Economic Cooperation: Report to the Australian Government*. Canberra: Australian National University, 1985.

————. *Australia and Pacific Economic Cooperation: Second Report to the Australian Government*. Canberra: Australian National University, 1987.

"New Steps Toward Building PECC Planned," *Pacific Economic Cooperation* (United States National Committee for Pacific Economic Cooperation) (Fall 1987).

Okita, Saburo. "Japan and the Pacific Basin," *Journal of International Affairs* 37 (Summer 1983): 13–20.

————. "Japan's Role in Pacific Basin Cooperation — Present and Future," *Euro-Asia Business Review* 4 (February 1985): 37–38.

————. "The Outlook for Pacific Cooperation and the Role of Japan," *The Indonesian Quarterly* 15 (July 1987): 494–505.

*Pacific Community Newsletter* (Pan-Pacific Community Association, Inc., Washington), various, 1981–84.

*Pacific Economic Community Statistics 1986*. Tokyo: PBEC Japan Member Committee, 1986.

*Pacific Economic Cooperation* (United States National Committee for Pacific Economic Cooperation), various, 1985– .

Pacific Economic Cooperation Conference. *Pacific Economic Outlook.* Washington, D.C.: U.S. National Committee for Pacific Economic Cooperation, 1989.

Pacific Economic Cooperation Conference. Ad Hoc Task Force on Institutional Development, *Report,* April 1989.

*Pacific Trade and Development Conference Newsletter* (PAFTAD Secretariat Canberra), various after 1984.

PBEC Reports on Annual Meetings, 1978 and later.

Schott, Jeffrey J. *More Free Trade Areas?,* Policy Analyses in International Economics 27. Washington, D.C.: Institute for International Economics, 1989.

Shishido, Toshio, and Ryuzo Sato. *Economic Policy and Development: New Perspectives (Essays in Honor of Dr. Saburo Okita).* Dover, Mass.: Auburn House, 1985.

Soesastro, Hadi, and Han Sung-Joo (eds.). *Pacific Economic Cooperation: The Next Phase.* Jakarta: Centre for Strategic and International Studies, 1983.

"Sydney Meeting, Pacific Basin Committee: A Report on the First General Meeting, 9-10 May 1968," *SRI-International* 6 (July 1968).

Tan, Augustine H.H., and Basant Kapur (eds.). *Pacific Growth and Financial Interdependence.* Sydney: Allen and Unwin, 1986.

Thakur, Ramesh, and Carlyle A. Thayer (eds.). *The Soviet Union as an Asian Pacific Power: Implications of Gorbachev's 1986 Vladivostok Initiative.* Boulder, Col.: Westview Press, 1987.

United Nations Economic and Social Commission for Asia and the Pacific. *Economic and Social Survey of Asia and the Pacific.* Annual.

United States. Congress. Joint Economic Committee. *Pacific Region Interdependencies: A Compendium of Papers.* Washington, D.C.: U.S. Government Printing Office, 1981.

————. Library of Congress. Congressional Research Service. "An Asian-Pacific Regional Economic Organization: An Exploratory Concept Paper." Prepared for the Committee on Foreign Relations, United States Senate. U.S. Government Printing Office, Washington, D.C., July 1979.

————. National Committee for Pacific Economic Cooperation. *Japan-U.S. Relations and the Pacific Basin.* San Francisco, 1987.

————. U.S. Information Service. "Baker Outlines Framework for Future Pacific Partnership." *Wireless File*, June 26, 1989.

Wanandi, Jusuf. "ASEAN and Pacific Basin Economic Co-operation." In Hiroshi Matsumoto and Noordin Sopiee (eds.). *Into the Pacific Era: Southeast Asia and Its Place in the Pacific.* Kuala Lumpur; Tokyo: Institute of Strategic and International Studies; Association of Promotion of International Cooperation, 1986, pp. 25–32.

————. *Security Dimensions of the Asia Pacific Region in the 1980s.* Jakarta: Centre for Strategic and International Studies, 1979.

Whitlam, E. Gough. *A Pacific Community.* Cambridge, Mass.: Harvard University Press, 1981.

Woods, Lawrence T. "Diplomacy and International Nongovernmental Organizations: A Study of the Pacific Economic Cooperation Movement." Doctoral Dissertation, Australian National University, 1988.

The following periodicals are particularly useful. Issues for certain years are cited as having articles on Pacific institutional ideas or developments.

*Asia Pacific Community*, mainly 1979–85 issues.

*Far Eastern Economic Review*, general, but see especially June, July, and November 1989 issues.

*Indonesia Quarterly*, mainly 1983–87 issues.

*Pacific Community*, mainly 1969–1974 issues.

Also note the following periodicals:

*Asian Survey* (United States)

*International Journal* (Canada)

*Journal of International Affairs* (Japan).

*Korea and World Affairs* (South Korea).

# Members of the
# C.D. Howe Institute[*]

---

[*] The views expressed in this publication are those of the author and do not necessarily represent the opinions of the members of the Institute.

Les Placements T.A.L. Ltée.
Placer Dome Inc.
Portfolio Management Corporation
Power Corporation of Canada
Prairie Pools Inc.
Pratt & Whitney Canada Inc.
Price Waterhouse & Co.
J. Robert S. Prichard
Procor Limited
ProGas Limited
Provigo Inc.
Quebec and Ontario Paper
    Company Limited
RBC Dominion Securities Inc.
Redpath Industries Limited
Simon S. Reisman
Henri Remmer
Retail Council of Canada
Grant L. Reuber
R.T. Riley
Robin Hood Multifoods Inc.
Rogers Communications Inc.
Rothschild Canada Inc.
The Royal Bank of Canada
Royal Insurance Company of
    Canada
Royal LePage Limited
Royal Trust
St. Lawrence Cement Inc.
Sandwell Inc.
Saskoil
Guylaine Saucier
André Saumier
The Hon. Maurice Sauvé
Sceptre Investment Counsel
Sceptre Resources Limited
ScotiaMcLeod Inc.
Sears Canada Inc.
Anthony A. Shardt
Sharwood and Company

Shell Canada Limited
Sherritt Gordon Limited
Sidbec-Dosco Inc.
Smith, Lyons, Torrance, Stevenson
    & Mayer
Le Soleil
Southam Inc.
Standard Life Assurance Company
Stikeman, Elliott, Advocates
Strategico Inc.
Sun Life Assurance Company of
    Canada
Suncor Inc.
Swiss Bank Corporation (Canada)
Teck Corporation
Téléglobe Canada
Thomson Newspapers Limited
3M Canada Inc.
The Toronto Dominion Bank
Toronto Star Newspaper Limited
The Toronto Stock Exchange
TransAlta Utilities Corporation
TransCanada PipeLines Limited
Trimac
Trizec Corporation Ltd.
Robert J. Turner
Unilever Canada Inc.
Urgel Bourgie Limitée
Manon Vennat
Ventures West Management
VIA Rail Canada Inc.
J.H. Warren
Tom M. Waterland
West Fraser Timber Co. Ltd.
Westcoast Energy Inc.
George Weston Limited
M.K. Wong & Associates Ltd.
Wood Gundy Limited
Xerox Canada Inc.
Zurich Life Insurance of Canada

## Honorary Members

W.J. Bennett

G. Arnold Hart

David Kirk

Paul H. Leman

A.M. Runciman

J. Ross Tolmie, Q.C.